My Journey
TO THE ENDS OF THE EARTH

Ivan N. Raley

WESTBOW
PRESS®
A DIVISION OF THOMAS NELSON
& ZONDERVAN

WestBow Press books may be ordered through booksellers or by contacting:

WestBow Press
A Division of Thomas Nelson & Zondervan
1663 Liberty Drive
Bloomington, IN 47403
www.westbowpress.com
1 (866) 928-1240

Scripture taken from the King James Version of the Bible.

Scripture taken from the New King James Version®. Copyright © 1982
by Thomas Nelson. Used by permission. All rights reserved.

ISBN: 978-1-9736-7984-4 (sc)
ISBN: 978-1-9736-7986-8 (hc)
ISBN: 978-1-9736-7985-1 (e)

Library of Congress Control Number: 2019918583

Print information available on the last page.

WestBow Press rev. date: 12/18/2019

Dedication

This book is dedicated to Carole A. Raley, my wife for more than 25 years. Without her help, encouragement, tender push from time to time, these stories would still be in my computer.

About the Author

It was a Friday morning in August 1953 when I knelt at the front on the sawdust floor at the open chapel at Camp Linden. I said to God in front of my friend and mentor, Jim Allen, "I will do whatever you want me to do, go through any door, and be whatever you want me to be." Never in my wildest dreams did I think that I would spend my life in His service; serve as Vice President of the Tennessee Baptist Children's Home for 12 years; and as an old man, continue to pastor & preach (as I have for the last 65 years) and love each moment of the journey.

After completing my education in the public schools of Jackson and Union University, I entered the United States Navy and spent my first two years in school at San Diego. While serving in the Navy I also served as Associate Pastor of the Balboa Park Baptist Church.

Only God could open the doors that would lead me to be a guest of the congressional speaker at the National Day of Prayer in the Cannon Office Building in our nation's capital. And to be a guest Chaplain at the United States House of Representatives; as well as opening the session with prayer and spend time with two different Speakers of The House.

After completing my service in the Navy a church in Tennessee called me as their pastor and I returned to the Volunteer state, the place I have called home for the remainder of my life. I was privileged to pastor five churches in Tennessee with at least one in each grand division.

I was also called to serve in disaster relief programs in the United States; in Venezuela, Honduras, Guatemala and Belize.

In 1994 I spent five months with the Southern Baptist Mission Board in Belize; and in the summer of '94 I was assigned to the countries of Rwanda and The Congo during the Civil war in Rwanda.

It was in 1994 that Carole and I joined our blended families. We were called to Brentwood where I served as Vice President of the Tennessee Baptist Children's Home.

Following the disaster of 9/11 in 2001, I was called to serve as a relief

Chaplin for the Fire Dept. of New York City, an experience which marked me forever.

My first book, "Just a Moment" had totaled what I thought was the sum of "an old life". Yet God continues to bless and care for me. My wife and our blended family have added joy and length to my years.

The Spirit of the Lord God is upon me, because the Lord has anointed me to preach good tidings unto the meek; He hath sent me to bind up the broken-hearted, to proclaim liberty to the captives and the opening of the prison to those who are bound.
Isaiah 61:1(KJV)
Ivan
pastoriraley@gmail.com
Also live at **www.kingofkingsradio.com**
Sundays at 11:00AM (Central Time)

Acknowledgments

To Brenda J. Hale, my sister-in-law, who read through most of the 1,200 stories I have written. Then she worked to edit, correct and arrange those for this book; her countless hours of work & assistance can never be repaid.

To the First Baptist Church of Byrdstown, who has allowed me to be their pastor for these past 17 years; who listened to these yarns and still returned for more, I am grateful.

To the Pickett County Press newspaper in Byrdstown, TN, who has published many of my stories weekly, I am also grateful.

To all seven of the churches where I had at the honor to pastor over my 65 years of preaching, I am truly blessed & grateful.

Most of all to my Savior & Lord, Jesus Christ, who has blessed me, opened doors I never dreamed I would walk through, and led me on this incredible journey to the end.

January

A New Year

On My Way to the Ends of the Earth

n Saturdays, 'The Old Man' always sat in front of the five-and-dime store, begging nickels, dimes & quarters from those who passed his way. The folks who saw him aren't sure how he got there most mornings because he didn't seem to have a soul who cared. The Old Man was always there, drawn over in a wheelchair, with his hand out. You could count on it.

Saturday was the day the boy got to come downtown with a few friends. They came to watch a black & white movie at the theatre on Main Street in Jackson, Tennessee.

The Old Man was ridiculed by most of the kids because he was so pitiful. On that first Saturday encounter, The Old Man yelled, "Hey, Boy!" It scared the boy half to death, because he knew the Old Man was talking to him. The boy didn't really know how to handle it at the time. The boy still has a hard time trying to get some folks to understand how it all happened. The Old Man could look smack through the boy's chest to see a heart very big and very tender.

The Old Man yelled again, "Hey Boy!" The boy couldn't figure out how The Old Man had somehow picked him out of the crowd. The boy walked across the street where the Old Man was parked in front of the store as usual. The Old Man motioned for the boy to lean down because he had something to say, "Push me to the alley behind Joe's Pool Hall," trying hard to whisper.

"Do what?" The boy was too scared to ask an intelligent question, and too concerned for the Old Man to run.

"You heard me. Now get me to the alley. I've got to go," the Old Man said with a sense of urgency in his voice. The boy pushed the Old Man out behind Joe's Pool Hall. The boy did it again the next Saturday; and the next, and the next.

The boy was afraid someone would think he was his own dad: dirty, unkempt, and it embarrassed him. They never talked much. There wasn't much that needed saying.

The movie house is now long gone from Jackson's Main Street. The Old Man is gone too, as well as Joe's Pool Hall. The story of how the Old Man got to his makeshift bathroom though is still very much alive. The story of the Old Man who needed a push; and the boy who was on his way to the ends of the earth.

On my trip to Venezuela for a revival in the village, we had a great first night when several people were saved. I walked out to the front yard of the church. A little boy, who had been saved, asked me if I would tell his father about Jesus. I assured him that I would and to bring his dad to church the next evening.

The little boy said his dad would not come to the church, but he would meet me the next day and take me to his house. I arranged for a young man to interpret for me. We all met at the church the next day and we were off to tell a man about Jesus. We went through the alleys, dumps, and trash and then we turned onto his street.

There it was. Joe's Pool Hall, and his father, an aged man locked in a wheelchair, dirty, unkempt, like the Old Man from my childhood in Jackson. My eyes filled with tears as I opened my Bible and introduced him to Jesus. That Friday night before I flew home, we filled a large feeder trough with water and baptized him, wheelchair and all.

My firm belief is, had not pushed the Old Man in Jackson, I would have never gone to Venezuela and a hundred other places I have been privileged to preach the good news of Jesus on my way to the ends of the earth.

What to Do

The old year has closed and nothing we do stops that. The New Year is here and likewise, we are helpless to hold it off. So what to do?

For the old year, we can only ask our heavenly Father to forgive all of the things we should have done but left undone. Not enough time, got started too late, didn't plan well. Spent more on ourselves than we had planned, so we had to cut back on gifts we would have liked to make, and the list goes on, as long as you can stay on your knees.

For The New Year, begin right now by giving it to Lord. Take out a new calendar of the New Year and now, write across each month, "I give this month to Jesus."

Put a mark on the Sundays in January and give each of them to Christ. See a birthday, or a special event? Pledge to write a card expressing your love and appreciation for the couple or individual.

Plan family time, vacation, something fun. Each time ask the Lord to direct the project and to prepare you to follow the leadership of the Holy Spirit.

Look at your budget and ask the Lord what you should do about your giving plan.

You know, I think we are off to a good start. Now make it real. Make it happen as you follow the leadership of the Holy Spirit, not just on Sundays, but on all the days of The New Year. See you in church Sunday.

A Throwaway

This had been the worst day of her sixteen years of life. Joyce knew it was about to get tragic. Her brother and sister left the dinner table. Her mother fixed a piece of pie and placed it on a plate in front of her. Her father filled his plate with the second load of spaghetti.

Then Joyce dropped the bomb. She was going to have a baby. The reaction was worse than she could have believed. Her dad threw his whole plate of spaghetti into the sink. He began to shout as if he were in his Sunday pulpit. Her mother simply plowed her head into her hands and began weeping.

Her father told her all the disgrace she had brought to her family. He said he had always known that she was a miserable sinner, and now she had brought ruin to him and all the family. He screamed at her, how he was in line to be the president of their state religious convention. "All is ruined!" he screamed. Most likely, he would lose his church because of her and the wicked choices she had made.

Nothing was ever mentioned as to anything that concerned her and her future. Joyce knew more than he did, how she had failed. She had not only broken God's plans, but hers as well. It was a moment in her life when she just got everything mixed up. All her emotions drove her and now, this.

For two days, she was not allowed to attend school. Her father said she would probably brag to all her friends about 'having a baby', no school and no contact.

Silence filled the house except when her father ranted and raved at her, called her names and accused her of the total breakdown of the family.

On the third day, he told her he thought best to get rid of "it". In spite of his best judgment, he was sending her to live with his older sister, who lived across the country in California. She was instructed to have the baby and then give it away. Maybe then he would allow her to return and finish school, but he didn't think so.

Joyce's aunt had been kind. Her own children were grown, so the aunt took care of Joyce. Also, her aunt saw that the baby had a good chance to be born healthy. Her father flew out the day after she gave birth. He brought a lawyer with papers for her to sign, but she refused. Joyce would not give him away. She would keep her son.

The father left in a rage and that was the last time she saw him. Her aunt allowed her to stay with her and helped with her son. Joyce finished school and her boy blossomed. After her graduation, she went to work full time. When her aunt died, her aunt's children asked her to move, so she had gone to a housing project.

Joyce's life was miserable with hard work and little reward. Her son was wonderful. They had moved from one housing project to another. Then at age seventeen, her son had been killed in a drive-by shooting. The community helped her bury him. She found herself in the bottom of a great pit, from which she never recovered.

Now, twenty years later, she was dying of cancer, in a hospital ward with three other women. Only the pleasant memory of her boy, who moved across her mind, brought any joy or peace to her.

Her father had gotten his wish. He had been the state president. Her mother had written her once but said she would not do so again.

Joyce felt the darkness of the room overtake her. She knew that she had made a mistake long ago. She also knew that she loved and trusted God. She would soon see both God and her son.

The young man walked down the hall of the hospital. The further he went, the more he knew that she would be in the worst part of the facility. The nurses all looked at the tall, handsome man about to approach his forties, and wondered who he could be. They had never seen him before. He walked into the room, sat down in the chair beside Joyce's bed, and took her hand in his.

He touched her brow, pressed his finger to her lips, then leaning over said, "Mom, it's me, Robert. I have come to take you home. Come on, Mom. It is time we both got out of this place." They walked hand in hand out of the building, unnoticed by anyone.

They were going home.

Pleased or Displeased

When I was a boy, we played a game called 'Pleased or Displeased'. It was a fun little game, in which each person would say if they were happy or not. Then one person would ask what it would take for them to be happy. They always said something silly like, "I would be pleased if Ivan would walk with Betty around the outside of the house." So Betty and I would walk around the house. Big deal, but it was fun. We all had a chance to make someone do something special.

Life is not really that simple today. I see so many people who are not pleased. You can tell by the way they drive, they are unhappy. Their voice is a giveaway, even the way they walk. If you know a person well, you can tell by their eyes, 'they are not happy.'

We live in such a wonderful world and such a great country. My house is heated and cooled; in fact I have used both on the same day. My bed is soft. The TV gets so many stations that by the time I flip through, it is time to get up. The doctor is down the street from me. I even have a membership in a Chopper service and they will take me to the hospital in Nashville, if it is needed. Not bad. My bathroom is inside the house. I have too many clothes, and my health for my age is just about right.

Is everything as I would like for it to be? Of course not, but when I stand and gaze into the 'Far off country', I see so many people who have nothing of the things I count as common. In Africa, no floors in the house, water five miles away, and doctors, who knew. The same was true in Central and South America. By their standards, I am a rich man.

Now in truth, this is not what brings me real pleasure. Yes, these things all contribute. What gives me real pleasure and real peace is that I know God loves me and that His Son gave Himself for me. Now that is worth an eternity.

A Spiritual Awakening in America

No matter who leads the nation, if God is not in control, there is no future. One thing about our system of government: we are able to take change in leadership, without falling apart. Our system allows us to get mad, to change parties, and to make great declaration. However, rarely does any real change occur.

I join you and others across our country and pledge my prayers to all of those who will be elected to serve in leadership positions. I pray not for a political change but a spiritual awakening in America.

We are too divided, too polarized, and too angry to become the Nation we should be in this world of the final time and coming kingdom. We need God. We see through the elements that God is still in control. He is not only the designer of this world; He is also the judge of this world.

Let us as individuals bring back the America that put 'In God We Trust" on our money. That America that proclaims for all to hear when we give our pledge of allegiance, 'One Nation under God.'

Our greatest hope, and our greatest weapon in doing this, is the life that each of us live as Christians, as men and women of real character. Let us not be angry with one another. Let us instead bring others to Jesus, not by what we say and preach, but by what we do and how we live. Let us be salt to our nation and light to our world, and let us be in that, ourselves.

The Failure of Fear

*"He shall not be afraid of evil tidings;
his heart is fixed, trusting in the Lord." Psalm 112:7 (KJV)*

In these trouble times with all of our fears, I must believe, "Stop being so afraid, believe God; He is going to win."

I have suffered from fear since I was a small boy. There was the fear of failure, missing the ball, not doing as well as others, and a thousand other fears. It was a very crippling destructive problem in my life. I always felt inferior, not prepared, and just not able to do the job.

This weight came to light when I was in the Navy. I was so fearful of failure that I could not perform. I worried about each detail until my mind was so cluttered with the fear that I just wanted to throw in the towel.

A Chief at San Diego saw this in me and said, "Ivan with your fear of failure, you are never going to be able to do enough, just to get through. Would it not be better to give it your best shot and see how it goes? If you fail, at least you tried. If you don't try, then you have already failed."

The Chief was right.

Moments in the Master's Land

Now and then, life gives to us one of those moments for which we have longed. As a boy, it was a simple fishing trip with my Dad, fishing from a boat near Pickwick Dam, or spending the night at my grandparent's house in Dyersburg.

Later, it was standing dressed in United States Navy blues, receiving the honors, as our colors were marched on the parade field before us.

For the first six days of our trip to Israel, we stayed in Tiberius on the shore of the Sea of Galilee. While the city is only mentioned once in the Bible, the sea served as a central part of Jesus' ministry.

While I sat in the dark one night, I listened as the waters of the sea lapped against the wall which protected our hotel from erosion. Far across on its eastern shore, I saw the lights of Jordan. On the sea itself, I saw fishing boats searching for their catch, in the light of the full moon.

Somewhere near, I wondered if it was where Jesus took a boat across to the other side to teach the people. Maybe it was close by that He walked to His disciples as they trembled in their boat during a storm. Somewhere on that sea, Jesus had slept in a boat while his disciples feared for their lives because of the storm.

It was here that He told them where to cast their nets so that they would have fish aplenty. From this sea, He called a fish to bring Him a coin so that He might pay his taxes. By this sea in His resurrected body, He prepared breakfast for His disciples. He told them in the early morning hours to cast over there for a great school of fish. Then He said to drag the nets full of fish to shore and join him in a seaman's breakfast.

Looking across that great sea, I could almost hear the Master saying, "Follow me and I will make you become fishers of men." Mark 1:17 (NKJV)

Our Nation needs to hear this calling.

Sharpener of Lives

"As iron sharpens iron, so a man sharpens the countenance of his friend." Proverbs 27:17 (NKJV)

Wonderful people whom I have met have sharpened my life. I will be forever grateful to each of them and pray that somehow I might sharpen the life of another.

It is not always the great and the powerful that help to shape the life of another. Sometimes it is janitor at a church, who has a great spirit of Jesus. Ones who shared that spirit with a young boy, who would drop by and just spend time asking questions. Another was a pretty girl, who lived across the street, was nice and kind to a fellow, who was not the best choice nor the best looking.

The sharpeners might be a little 'old' couple who lived across the street and spent countless hours answering the unimportant questions of a child.

Then there was a deacon and his wife at Calvary Church, who impressed the young man with their lives. 'Sonny' came to love the friends of his parents, Mrs. Simmons and Cletus.

There are also giants along the way, men like Dr. Stow, with whom it was a joy to ride down the interstate. I listened to his voice and his heart, as he poured out truths about life and Jesus. Another giant was a houseparent, who dedicated his life to give to those whom much of the world think of as "a throw away", to give them another chance, a real chance for a good life. Then there was a social worker, program director, and far too many to name, who gave me insight into life and the other side of the story.

How about a deacon in the church, who protected me from a member concerned that the kids and I were going to wear out the grass in the church yard playing football. The deacon's response to the upset member was, "If I have to choose between grass and kids, I think I will come down on the side of kids." The nice twist to that story was that the same man, who had such concerns for the grass, made it possible for us to purchase eight acres in the back that made a perfect place to play for kids.

I could spend weeks just calling names, seeing faces, and remembering moments where others have touched and sharpened my life.

Don't worry about your position in the world. Just make sure your position with Jesus is secured and you, too, will be a sharpener of lives for Him.

Did It Snow!

ow, it was beautiful! They said it would snow and it did. Then I got out of my house, tried to drive in it, and almost didn't get home. This was on Friday, so I was stuck at home for the rest of the time.

Now those who know me, know that I don't keep food in my house. I had stopped at B and K's Store, got a loaf of bread, some butter spread, a pack of cheese, lunch meat, bacon that you cook in the microwave, and a couple of cans of soup. I was ready.

As I prepared my first meal, I toasted a couple of pieces of bread, put some butter on, then put on a slice of cheese and lunch meat. I looked at the ketchup I had and it had expired in February of 2015. Not good. Jelly had expired in 2014, with sandwich spread that expired in July 2015.

I threw them all away and decided I liked just meat and cheese on my bread. Not bad, but not good. Also there was no one to talk to, no one with whom I could simply place an order for my food, or talk to while I ate. There was no bill to pay and no tip to leave. It just did not seem like much of a meal.

I did notice that the packs of lunch meat I had chosen were only enough for just one sandwich. Well, so much for cooking. The soup wasn't bad, but still a lot was missing. Where were Russell and Johnnie and all the others?

Not good. It was Saturday and I could not get out of my garage. Then came Sunday. I got the bacon and it wasn't bad.

With my dog, Max looking on, like he was starving, it didn't last long. Sunday, I am supposed to preach! With a foot of snow on the parking lot, most people like me were stuck in their drives. I was lost.

I even felt guilty for not being in church. Then my friend, David Rich called, and wanted to know if I needed anything. Well, I first said no, but then I realized he was sincere. I said, "Yes!" He came in his four wheel drive and we were off to the Shell Restaurant, to have a morning biscuit with egg, cheese and bacon. It was wonderful.

Then we stopped at the grocery store. I got Max some treats and myself some jelly. Wow, I am going to make it!

On the way back to my house, we passed a large field covered in the wonderful, white snow. It was just perfect, no mark, no footprints, just beautiful. David said to me, "Pastor isn't that beautiful? That is just the way our sins will look when we get to Heaven, as white as snow, new fallen snow."

That made my day! All has been well, since that nice gesture on his part to take me to the store, and see the wonder of God! Thanks, David.

February

Agapé Love

A Valentine Letter

As I closed my front door to make the short walk over to my church office, I noticed an out of state car parked in our cemetery parking area. Having some extra time, I decided to meet the people in the car. As I rounded the church where the cemetery was in clear view, I noticed only one person standing by a grave, about half way down the cemetery.

As I approached, he noticed me, turned, and introduced himself. He looked to be about my age, at that time in my late thirties. I spoke my name and told him that I was the pastor of the church.

Noticing the grave where he stood, I asked if it was a relative. "No", he said, "Just an old friend." Seeing the age on the marker, I said, "At 23, not very old." "No," he said, "Just from a long time ago."

With this, tears welled up in his eyes. I asked if he wanted to talk about it. Now as the tears began to wash down his face, he told me that they dated in college. When he had left for 'Nam, she promised to wait for him.

After a long pause, he said, "I got the letter that she had been killed in a car wreck on Valentine's Day." He said he was deep in the jungle when the letter from her parents reached him. He couldn't get home and by the time he left 'Nam, her family had moved back to Florida. This was his first visit to the grave.

I discovered that he had never married, remained in the Army, and was planning on retiring in a few years. He just wanted to see her grave before he returned to Texas, where he was stationed.

I told him to take all the time he needed, put my hand on his shoulder and thanked him for serving our country and left for my office.

He called to me and said, "Preacher does the hurt ever go away?"

I stopped, shook my head "no" then responded, "It gets better. This visit will help, but true love is never forgotten, never."

A Good Day

We listened to a special presentation in our high school gym yesterday, as a real American hero spoke to students, and shared events from February 23, 1945.

At 5' 6" tall, Hershel 'Woody' Williams was first turned down for Marine Corps service. Trying again and again, he was accepted.

On February 23, he found himself on an island of Japan, Iwo Jima. He was on the front battle lines. Of 279 men in his unit, 262 had been killed or put out of action by wounds, too severe to let them serve. By his own bravery and through many unguarded returns to the supply line, he took seven enemy pill boxes out of commission, allowing tanks and marines to advance.

Look up his name and deeds, for which he received the Medal of Honor. He is the last living Marine, who received the medal in that battle of ash, rocks, blood and death. He is the stuff of what this nation is made.

With great pride, our staff and student body stood up, and gave him their full attention. Tom, at Sunset Marina, had something to do with all the plans, so my hat is off to him and his duty as a concerned citizen. Folks, complain if you like, but we have great heroes from every community.

Iwo Jima

*I*n 1945, five Marines and one Navy Corpsman raised the flag on Mount Suribachi on Iwo Jima. Joe Rosenthal took the picture, which has become one of the most famous of World War II. Monuments around the country have been made from that famous moment captured by Rosenthal.

Sergeant Mike Strank, the leader of the group and the oldest at age 26, died along with Harlon Block on that bloody island on March 1, 1945. Franklin Sousley died on March 21. The survivors were Ira Hayes, a Pima Indian, along with Rene Gagnon who survived the battle and returned to the U. S. as heroes of the battle. Navy Corpsman John Bradley was originally named as the sixth man. [In 2016, the Marines corrected the names to include Harold Henry Schultz as the sixth man.] None of the men considered themselves heroes. They all spoke simply of doing what they were told to do.

The battle, which was planned for one week, lasted five weeks where 6,800 Marines died, and more than 20,000 others were wounded. The Japanese lost 18,844 of their 22,000 men. This was the only battle in which the American causalities were greater than the enemies.

These almost seven thousand men, who never came off that rock of blood and bodies, paid the ultimate price for the freedoms, which you and I enjoy, and take for granted today. Let us deserve their sacrifice, let us pass on to those who follow us, the dreams and hopes of those boys, lest we dishonor their payment for our privilege.

America is the greatest country in the world. There is no argument about that. The greatness was grown from the lives of young men, who never grew into real adulthood, who died as boys because their country needed their sacrifice, for our freedoms.

It Was a Shack

About a dozen of us had gathered to watch the home burn. We had called the fire department. We were so far out, and too far from a source of water for it to do any good, so we just stood there and watched the chicken-coop of a house vanish in the flames.

I told the men standing there that I would go into town and get the couple who lived in the house. It was Saturday and I was sure they were in town doing a little shopping. Someone asked if I was going to put them in my car.

I turned, I am sure, with a frown on my face and said, "Sure, why not?" Another man called out, "They are so dirty! Besides this wasn't a fit place for anyone to live."

I said, "But it was their place. To them, it was home. Remember how you felt last winter when your garage burned, John?" I said, as I reached my car. "Wasn't much of a building but it was yours." They got real quiet and watched as I drove away.

I found the couple. They fell onto me and wept like small children, when I told them about the house. I held them, then got them to my car. As I was coming around to get in the driver's seat, the mayor stopped me. He told me to bring them to an empty house the city had. He said he would take care of the paper work.

The owner of the furniture store said he would take some furnishings out for them to have. Another merchant said he had some clothes, and he would bring them over.

The grocery store owner said he would add to their buggy and bring some food over.

The community responded and the last was better than the first. Later, the editor of the newspaper wrote a story about it. He said the unnamed preacher had paid for it all. He said the town saw the preacher hug the couple, and let them fall in tears on him.

That wasn't so. It happened because people saw others hurting and felt the hurt and tears and sorrow.

He Noticed

Mrs. Morton had lived alone for a very long time. Her last relative had died more than 20 years earlier. Few, if any people, even knew that she was alive. No one came to visit, the phone seldom rung, and her sofa had not been used for a number of years.

Now she was sick, and life was fleeing. There was no one who knew and no one who cared.

Brittany, a twelve year old Girl Scout, knocked on her door. Hearing a faint 'come in', Brittany opened the door and stepped into a dark, stale entrance. She saw the small, frail woman sitting alone by the window in the living room.

Mrs. Morton spoke softly and said, "Come in, child, what I can do for you?" Brittany moved cautiously into the room and told her that she was selling Girl Scout Cookies. The lady nodded and asked her the price of a box. Brittany answered and watched as she opened the bag on the table beside her and took out the money.

It seemed to take her a very long time. They talked a minute and Brittany left. The next day she remembered the elderly lady and went back to visit. This happened on a regular basis for the next several months. Mrs. Morton discovered a wonderful friend in the young girl.

Brittany would sometimes bring her flowers and always asked if she needed for her to do some chore before she left. Mrs. Morton would always hug her and say that the nurse, who came three times a week, would bring her everything she needed.

Sometimes Brittany would cry all the way back to her house thinking about how sad it must be to live all alone. One last time, Brittany visited, to discover the door ajar and Mrs. Morton was on the floor deceased.

When the state packed up Mrs. Morton's belongings, they found a note. Mrs. Morton said that her greatest moments in life had been those spent with a twelve year old girl named Brittany. The world never noticed the loving spirit of Brittany, but Mrs. Morton noticed, and so did God.

Hurt Is Real

This was a new world for Richard, as new as if he were in some foreign land. He got out of his car, noticed on the outside it looked better than any on the lot. He knew that under the steel and fiberglass, it was being held together more by prayer and will than anything. Previously Richard had the car serviced as soon as he expected a problem. Now, it was when it would not go any farther, that he scraped the money together. It had been a very upscale car, when he had spent most of his time in it, running from appointment to appointment. The appointments had ended almost two years ago. Now he just cleaned and washed his car each week. What else did he have to do?

Inside the state employment office, Richard took a number and waited. The company, where he had invested twenty years of his life, had made a mistake which cost them all of their assets and his job, along with another thousand people. They had managed to give him a reasonable severance package, with the car and names of other companies in his business. As for his 401k plan, it was only the part leftover after the market fell.

The package was spent, insurance gone, car barely running, and he believed he was next. He had tried all the places he knew to try.

The kids who interviewed him just looked at him, like he was some kind of leftover relic from the past. Not even sixty years old yet, and already old, that's what he thought.

The lady who interviewed Richard at the state employment office said as for medical salesmen, his chances of finding any kind of job didn't exist. There were too many others like him, walking the streets, looking for a job.

Richard considered going back to school and getting a teacher's certificate. The local principal warned there were three people in line for every job. Richard checked medical training schools, who said, "They knew he would be great", after investing twenty thousand dollars. His friends in the field told him only about half of graduates got a job in their trained field. The pay was nothing close to what the school said. He left the office wondering where to go next. Maybe he would go home. At least there, he was still wanted and needed.

Richard drove by his church, and felt the greatest pain of all. After twenty years of being part of a church family, no one had ever mentioned his hurt or sense of "lost-ness". The pastor said he would pray for Richard. Richard knew that God did answer prayers. There, in his home of worship was no warmth, no assurance, not even an invitation to dinner.

Richard wasn't sure what to do next. They could reverse-mortgage the home, and maybe it would be enough to get to the end. Everyone said things were getting better at 710 Cole Street. This was not even close to being true.

Not even close. Hurt is real, so real and sometimes it seems to never end. Richard knew that God did answer prayers.

Spot and Charlie

Charlie had never expressed any emotion toward his mother, he spoke very little, did not want to be touched, and spent his life somewhere deep inside himself. Betty, his mother took him to school each day, but she wondered if it was only adding a burden to the teacher, Miss Rachel.

Each day, Miss Rachel greeted him like he was the only person in her class. Even with all the love she could give, Charlie lived somewhere in his own world.

About two months into the school year, Miss Rachel decided to bring a small fuzzy puppy to class. She had rescued the puppy from the dog pound. She called him Spot, because of the large black spot on his head, surrounded by an otherwise white body. Spot took immediately to Charlie. Spot raced across the room to where Charlie kept his world blocked from the others.

Charlie had nothing to do with Spot. Spot barked at him, tried to climb into his lap, but nothing doing for Charlie. The days turned to three weeks with Spot running each day to Charlie. Being rejected but staying close all the same, Spot watched Charlie like he was the only kid in the room. One day, when Spot jumped into Charlie's lap, instead of the usual rejection, Charlie touched him, and then held him. The days became weeks and the two grew a bond together that was a wonder to both his mother and teacher.

One night as Betty put Charlie to bed, she made her always rejected attempt to hug and kiss him good night. Charlie just stared at her and turned toward the wall, as was his normal reaction. Just as she went to close the door, she heard her son say, "Mommy, hug and kiss". She rushed back to the bed and found him receptive to her good night hug and kiss for the first time in his life.

As she reached for the phone to call and tell Miss Rachel, she realized that it was too late. Just the same, Betty let the phone ring. Both ladies wept and praised God for a tiny crack in the wall of silence.

The next day, Spot came to live with Charlie and the world began to be brighter. Hope was there. Maybe, just maybe, there was a brighter future for all of them.

All I Wanted

Everyone in town knew Mr. Sharp. Most of them knew that he was on his last visit to the hospital, but no one seemed to care. It wasn't that they didn't like him, they just did not know him and did not care one way or other.

Mr. Sharp had lived all of his 80 plus years in the county, never married, no relations to anyone that we knew. Just Mr. Sharp, that's who he was.

The old stooped man came to town on Saturday, got his supplies, and went back to the old house where he had spent a lifetime. "Old Stooped", that is what they called him and that's who he became.

Most people believed Mr. Sharp had money, but it was never evident by the way he lived. His car was ten years old, and his truck about the same. It had been even longer since his house had been painted.

At the Baptist Hospital in Memphis, I went to visit with Mr. Sharp. I had stopped by his home a number of times before. He was nice enough but it really never seemed to matter to him, one way or another. He never came to church, or never attended a funeral. He was just alone, always alone.

We talked a bit, Mr. Sharp knew that his time was limited. It didn't seem to bother him, and we talked of nothing.

After I tried to talk about his faith, and his coming death, he wasn't interested. I prayed, told him that I was leaving, then said, "Mr. Sharp, is there anything I can do for you, anything?" He said, no, all was well, then he said, "Preacher, thanks for coming to see me and thanks for praying for me. When you do my funeral, tell the people all that I ever wanted was for someone to hold me. They really wanted to, but I lived my life in such a way that no one ever wanted to. It was my fault. Tell them to be careful and to share themselves with others, and don't do like I did."

If you wish for someone to hold you, you really do need to be "hold-able".

Real Neighbors

The couple saw her walking on the side of the road as they drove by. It was cold, rainy and just a miserable day. John looked at his wife and she nodded, "Yes", so he pulled over. His wife asked the young lady if she would like a ride. She hesitated, but the weather was terrible, and she was so cold. She ran and opened the back door to get into the car.

John introduced himself to her, that he was the pastor of a small church just outside the city. John's wife told the young lady that she was Carla and asked where she was headed. The girl said her name was Nancy and she was on her way to work at the 'I-Hop' about a mile down the road.

It didn't take the couple long to discover that Nancy was a single girl from out of town, trying to make a living and start a new life. Nancy lived about three miles from the restaurant and walked to work six days each week.

Nancy had left home when her mother died. She was trying to begin a new life, with new friends, in new world, with a new direction. The direction was new but nothing else had worked. She was still determined.

John and Carla let her out at the restaurant, talked between them about her, then his wife prayed for Nancy while they drove home.

That night about eleven, Carla asked John if they should go to the restaurant and give Nancy a ride home. John agreed. Thus began a journey of six years which saw a young lady mature, get an education, fall in love with a great guy, marry, and start her own career and family.

Sure, there were setbacks and difficulties to overcome. Sure, there were times of almost giving up, disappointments, failure, and frustration. Then, there is nothing like having Real Neighbors.

March

Easter Time

Palm Sunday

They call this Sunday, "Palm Sunday", when Jesus came to Jerusalem. The people took Palm Tree branches and went out to meet Him. They cried, "Hosanna! Blessed is He who comes in the Name of the Lord! The King of Israel!" John 12:13 (NKJV)

Jesus knew that Friday was coming. Jesus washed His disciple's feet. He was the servant, He who was Divine, who placed the stars into space, who told the rivers where to flow, who pulled mountains from the deep, and who caused the Sun to shine. He was the servant.

Jesus told His Disciples that He was going to make a home for them. They were troubled because they did not know the way. Jesus said to them, "I am the way, the truth, and the life. No man comes to the Father except through Me." John 14:6 (NKJV)

Jesus knew that Friday was coming, and in spite of all of their words of loyalty, few would be there on Friday. He knew that those who had shouted Hosanna, would cry, "Crucify Him". Friday was coming.

Jesus loved us too much to turn back. He was beaten, made fun of, and hung like a common criminal on a cross. He did not turn back. He met the darkness of death for each of us. Paid our debt, forgave us and saved all who would come to the Father in His Name.

His love was not fickle. He loved with the very heart of God, for He was God.

Good Friday is Coming

The spit of the guards ran down his beard. His back bled with the crimson red of his blood, and his body exposed to the world. He was barely able to stand. It was Good Friday.

The crown of thorns placed on his head pained with every move. The people cheered, called him names, and called for his death. It was Good Friday.

The nails forever marked his hands and feet. These scars were carried even into eternity. His friend denied knowing him, his mother wept at the foot of the now raised cross. It was Good Friday.

The sun grew dark, the earth shook, the holy veil of the temple was torn, the Father's face was hid, and he cried in pain. It was Good Friday.

The debt He did not owe was paid. My debt, which I could not pay, was forgiven. It was Good Friday.

My Church

ur church was just across the street and a couple of houses down toward the east. It was always in sight of my home when I was growing up. As long as I can remember, that was my church.

My Dad said one Sunday morning, as we were all getting ready to go to church, he heard several cars blowing their horns on Lexington Avenue. He decided to go see what all the horn blowing was about. There I was, in all my Sunday-best, standing in the middle of Lexington, holding a stick in my hand, stopping all the traffic. Of course, it only took Dad a moment to realize the problem. He rushed into the street, picked me up, and on the way back to the house, asked what in the world was I doing. He said I told him that I wanted to be the first person in church that Sunday, so I decided to block the traffic, so no one got there before I did.

I guess we should have known then that I was going to become a pastor. I have always loved church. Mother said that after we moved to Lindsey Street, if we drove by the church and lights were on, I would pitch a fit because we were not there. It didn't matter if it was a ladies meeting, or a deacon's meeting, if someone was in church, I wanted to be in church.

I have wonderful memories of Calvary Church. As an old man, I can say for certain that they knew how to love a little boy there. There I made my profession of faith at the age of nine and was baptized. I preached my first sermon there when I was sixteen. I always wanted to pastor a church named Calvary. I said I would buy every billboard around and put on it, "Life Begins at Calvary, corner of Lexington and Tomlin."

The church moved some years after I left. I preached the last revival in the building and then took part in the first revival at their new building. When I visited one day about five years ago, it stirred up so many memories that I had to weep. For life did begin for me at Calvary, there at the corner of Lexington and Tomlin.

To all those who made it possible, I know they are all now in Glory. Thank you, thank you for knowing how to love a little boy.

Breakfast Long Ago

The morning light had begun to break through the sides of the truck, partly covered with canvas. It was our cabin for a night of camping on the Tennessee River.

I looked out the rear flap that had been folded back to let in the morning sun. I smelled the aroma of bacon cooking, coffee perking, and smoke from campfires moving across our campground.

I saw Dad bent over the fire tending the bacon. He looked across the still fog that covered the river. I was about nine when this warm and wonderful memory was carved into my soul. It had been a wonderful weekend with Dad, some of his friends, and their sons. Now we shared a campfire breakfast together.

I saw fish caught the night before as they got prepared for the fire. A couple of other fathers gathered to stretch, get a cup of coffee, and maybe cast a line for an early morning bite, by the fish of their dreams.

As my father cooked, I was delighted. It was one of my best mornings. It must have been the same type of morning on the sea, when the fishermen heard the call of Christ. He told them to cast on the other side of the boat and then bring some of their catch to have breakfast with Him.

The risen Christ had arrived early, prepared breakfast for his friends, and now waited for them to join Him. What a moment!

What a morning! Try breakfast with Jesus and do it soon.

What is Wrong

The ten mile drive, from my office to Steve's house, took almost thirty minutes because of the condition of the unkempt road. All the turns and twists, that were required on the road, gave me plenty of time to worry.

That is who I was then and to a large degree, still am. In spite of my knowledge of the Lord, and my faith in Him, I still worry. I kept trying to think why Steve called and asked me to come out to his home. Most of the time, they did not want visitors at his house. I think they were self-conscious of the way the house looked.

Steve did not provide even a hint of what it could be. I traveled down the road to the house, as well as down the road to any concern and problem I could imagine. Somewhere on that road, I left ten years of my life. You cannot believe how old I really am.

I saw the house and Steve was standing on the porch. I always believed the vines that grew up the sides of the house and around the walls, kept the house together more than the nails in the wood.

Steve walked out to my car and thus began the long story of a visit to the doctor by his wife. He told me the news that she had cancer and the journey to recovery was doubtful, long, and expensive.

There was no money for treatment, no insurance, and no certain cure even if funds were available. We prayed, we cried, and we prayed all the more. Their lives were shattered and my heart was broken.

To shorten the story, after a lot of prayer by our church, I called a doctor I had known in the Navy. He called someone else, they called another, and soon a free plan was laid out that just might bring recovery.

When I left the community, she had been cancer free for several months. Later, I received an old fashioned, handwritten letter that said it had been more than six years and all was well.

Years later, I ran into Steve at a truck stop on Interstate 40, when I was with the Baptist Children's Home. It was a joyful and happy unexpected reunion. His wife was gloriously well and life was a joy. He wanted to thank me but we both remembered that it was from the Lord, not from us.

I left the truck stop wondering why I had to suffer through my weakness. Why I just could not put it in The Hands that would bring the answer. I am still seeking that. I am finding about my eternity, but I do still worry about today. Man, I need to work on that.

By the Side of the Water

The last night I spent by the Sea of Galilee in Israel, I sat in a lawn chair facing out toward the open water. In the distance, you could see the lights of the Nation of Jordan, not very friendly toward Israel. Closer, scattered across the dark sea, you could see the lights of fishing boats on the Sea of Galilee.

As I let my mind wander across that dark water, I thought of the time long ago when Jesus stood on that shore. It was on that shore that He called some of His disciples. From that shore, He walked across the sea and calmed the storm for His friends. It was by that shore that He cooked breakfast for His disciples, before He left for glory. It was from that shore that He told them where to cast their nets so that they might catch a lot of fish. I think Jesus loved the water.

On this Monday, stand in your heart by the side of the water and cast all your fears into the water. In the time of crisis in our land, when all seems to be so fearful, let Christ take those fears and cast them to the bottom of the water and leave them there.

I Have Missed You So Much

The small boy stopped his crying and looked into his mother's eyes as she reached down, put her arms around him, and assured him that he was okay. For the briefest of moments, he had gotten lost in the large store and someone had seen him crying. They had called over the speaker for a 'lost mother.' The moment she had heard the call, she looked around and knew it was her son who was crying. She was the mother that was lost.

It was wonderful to see the way he looked at her, when she ran to him and knelt down to hold him. That is one of the great gifts of mothers, that warm and safe embrace. All of us have rejoiced, when we saw our child or another loved one, looking at us with those big bright eyes. There is just something about that look that reaches out and grabs our hearts.

Have you ever considered that God would love to see that same look on our faces as we bow before Him in prayer? Eyes bright with joy, heart filled with excitement, all because we were coming to see our Master in prayer.

Perhaps, we don't realize it, because the reason is we do not spend any time listening to God. Just listening in silence before Him, with eyes that are expecting and hearts filled with joy, when even our bodies need His strength.

We talk too much. We should listen more. Maybe we've never experienced it because we never seek Him with such a heart of wonder. Even my dog, Louie used to jump, bark, and get so excited when my car pulled in the drive.

Now we really should be smarter than dogs. We could certainly be more excited than they are when we meet our Master.

After all, real prayer is welcoming the Master home into our heart. I used to think that Louie was saying, "Where have you been? I've missed you so much."

I think Jesus would love for us to look at Him with that same longing desire to be held in His arms.

April

Spring Days

It Be OK

"Looking unto Jesus, the author and the finisher of our faith...."
Hebrews 12:2 (NKJV)

hile Tom was nearer my father's age than mine, in many ways he related to me as another twelve year old boy would. He liked things I liked: cowboy and Indian movies, baseball. We talked about all the things which most of my friends talked about.

Tom worked for my dad. When I was a boy, Tom came each week to pick up our trash, and work in the yard. All those years, he had been a good friend to my father, as well as to me.

The hospital staff told me Tom only had a few days left. I left my office early and went by his hospital room. He was alone, in a lot of pain, yet happy to see me. We had a moment enjoying old memories. Tom loved old western movies we had both watched when I was a boy. We talked about Roy Rogers, Gene Autry, Johnny Mac Brown, and many others. We talked about how little things cost back then. We said how much fun we had without the help of a phone, computer, or even a TV.

Tom knew that I understood he was very sick. I wanted him to know that I would pray for him. I asked if he had any decisions or thoughts he wanted to share, now would be the perfect time. Tom turned toward me and with dim eyes, said, "Sonny, it sure has been good to work all those years for Mr. Raley. I hate to think what my life would have been if I had not been able to work for him. He be a real good man, Sonny. Watching you grow up and become a preacher boy has been real good. I been keeping an eye on you and I am sure glad we had all those chats long ago. Now time be done come that I got other things to do, just like you got other places to be. Sonny, I be fixed my eyes on Jesus a long time ago. Like those old movies be ok. They always ended with good guys winning. I know my movie be alright, the ending will be good."

I prayed as I left, cried a bit for an old friend, and upon reaching my car said, "Thank You, Lord."

John Had It Right

John had worked for my dad all of my life. I never remembered going to the compress that John wasn't there. He often worked in our yard, was around a lot, visited my father when he was sick, and attended his funeral. I had preached in his church on a special Sunday and knew that he was a very involved servant of our Lord.

When his church decided to honor him, they invited me to be one of the guests and to say a few words about John.

You can imagine how I rose to the occasion. I put all the crowns I could on John. I sincerely thanked him for his friendship to my family and especially to my dad.

When John rose to speak, he said something like, "I be grateful to Mr. Ivan for them nice words but he be a lot nicer to me than I be worth. Now he be right, I did love Mr. Raley, but then all I ever did was what God 'spected me to do. I just do what be my job as a Christian."

John sure had it right.

Water

utside the camp in Zaire, Africa, I remember the lines of children who stood waiting, not for food but for a drink of clean water. About a thousand people a day would die because they were drinking bad water. They got cholera, which along with starving bodies, would kill them within a day or two.

The local government had not cleared us to let children into the new compound we had built for them. Even in a war torn country, there are people who rule and must have their way. Each morning, a number of volunteers would travel the streets of Goma to pick up the bodies of those who had died during the night.

We had finished the camp for 500 children, hired the workers, and were ready to receive the children. Some bureaucrat had to come and give us permission to save their lives.

Still the people slept along the fence, stood in the sun, and looked desperate throughout the day, waiting for water.

Three of us decided we could wait no longer. We ran water pipes through the fence. We let the water run freely, so that all who wished, could get lifesaving water.

More than three thousand people came with pans, buckets, anything which held water over the two days we allowed the water to run.

At last, the "powers to be" came and allowed us to open the camp and even to leave the water running through the fence.

Thirst was finished and defeated.

A Pillow for Jesus

C ome and lay your head in my lap, come and rest awhile with me. I will be so much the stronger to know that you found me worthy of just holding your head for even a moment.

I visited their home when I was stationed in San Diego. They were one of the older couples in our church at Balboa Park and always invited the sailors to go home with them for lunch on Sunday. The house was small and humble but neat and well appointed, a very welcome break from the sterile environment of the Navy quarters.

I noticed a beautiful, but well-worn pillow on a table in the hall. I asked what special meaning was attached to a pillow in such a place of honor.

The lady explained the first time she heard in the scripture that Jesus "had nowhere to lay His head*" that she went home and cried all night. Her mother, full of wisdom, got her this pillow and advised her to put it in the bed. Each night as she prayed, she told her to close her prayer by inviting Jesus to lay his head on the beautiful pillow. She said as she grew older, she knew that it was a bit crazy, but she always wanted Him to know He had a place in her heart. Wow, what a heart.

*(Luke 9:58 NKJV)

I Like Our Town

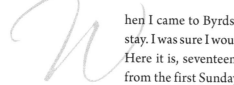hen I came to Byrdstown as a "ship in", I didn't come to stay. I was sure I would only be around two or three years. Here it is, seventeen years later, and that is a long time from the first Sunday in February, 2002.

People come from big cities like Nashville, with just a couple of credit cards. My first time in Byrdstown, I didn't bring any cash. A group of us went to lunch when suddenly I realized that they did not take credit cards. They also would not cash an out of town check, so I had to borrow ten dollars from Jack to get out of washing dishes for my lunch. Not really sure I ever paid that ten dollars to Jack. Maybe that it is why they have allowed me to stay so long, giving me time to pay back that first loan.

Everyone thought I would leave Byrdstown when I retired from the Baptist Children's Home in 2006. By that time, I had fallen in love with my new adopted home. Now I know time is getting short for me, but I still enjoy hanging on in this beautiful place.

Right here in Byrdstown, I have received the best medical care anyone could hope to receive. They know my name at the clinic and at a lot of the stores where I shop. I had rather pay a bit more if I can get it here, than to drive to some other place. Besides, they seem to appreciate my shopping.

Our school is great. Our teams have character and our people are real. Because I lived here, I opened Congress twice with prayer, which not many can say that. I attended the National Day of Prayer in Washington, D.C., opened our State House of Representatives twice, and spoke to the high school graduates. Life has been good to me.

You can be listen to our small church on five FM stations and on the internet around the world. Not bad for a small town, old man. That small church poured over $120 thousand dollars back into our community and missions around the world this past year. They are so unselfish.

Not sure about the last day, but today has been great, thank you.

A Fresh Sheet

During WWII, I started school. Like Americans everywhere, we tried to be as careful as we could with all of our school supplies. Thus, we wrote on all of the paper. We had our margins all the way out to the edge. We wrote on both sides of the sheet, saving all of the paper we could, so that we helped the war efforts.

Now and then, not often, but on a special project, the teacher would say, "Now students get out a fresh sheet of paper." I loved those days, just looking at that clean, fresh sheet of paper and dreaming of all the things I could do with it. That was magic.

Each week, our Lord is going to say to each of us, "The week has ended, it is now part of history, so get out a fresh sheet of paper and let's start a new week."

I am looking at my wonderful fresh sheet, yet unlived, unused, no marks, no mistakes, no do overs, just a brand new fresh week.

Just think, it will be what we place on it, our dreams, our hopes, our gifts to each other and all that our hearts can plan and do.

I wonder, will I love more, touch the lives of others more, help more, care more, show my devotion both to God and His creation? Will I be a better citizen, speak softer, give others the benefit of the doubt, judge less, let others see more of my love for them and our Lord?

You know I can and so can you. There is a fresh sheet of paper coming! Nothing on it to spoil it! I love fresh sheets.

Bobbie Jo

Bobbie Jo Carson stood on the beautiful green grass of the cemetery at the Asbury Methodist Church, near Arp community, west of Ripley, Tennessee. The lovely fall weather threw a blanket of peace and tranquility over the area.

Bobbie Jo could remember the April morning that she had waited for Pete Carson to board the City of New Orleans train, as it made its southbound journey to that famous city. From there, Pete would take a military train across the United States and find his ship, an LST, waiting for him in San Diego.

Mrs. Carson remembered how proud she was of Hospital Corpsman Third Class Pete Carson, as he stood there in his dress blues, waiting for the long journey to begin. They were so in love. Even the strangers who saw them knew their love.

In her hand, Mrs. Carson held all the letters they had exchanged and how she treasured each of them, as she looked over that green hill of memories. On that cold January day in 1945, Pete's dad had come to tell her that Pete would not come home. Pete's LST 460 had been hit by a Japanese Kamikaze plane. On December 21, 1944, at Mindoro Island, Philippines, Pete was one of the 27 men who didn't come home.

Bobbie Jo looked at the bronze plaque which the Navy had provided. It said, "Petty Officer 2nd Class Pete Carson, July 17, 1921 – December 21, 1944, Corpsman United States Navy.

Mrs. Carson said softly, "Pete, it is over. Japan surrendered, and most of your friends will be coming home. Honey, I loved you when you left, and I love you now. Rest in peace my love, and thank you for your gift to all of us, our freedom."

In Memory of 416,800 forces who did not return from World War II.

A Boy's Voice

Seaman Gill Maddox looked out across the beach at San Diego. The sun had placed its light beneath the surface of the western Pacific Ocean and the cool air of the summer night was blowing in from the far away ocean.

Gill's heart was broken. The letter that he carried in his pocket had closed the hope he had for a life with the girl of his dreams. Boot camp had not gone well. He knew he would love the Navy, but he hated it instead.

Gill had not made the school he had hoped for, and was only a few days from being placed on a ship, headed to sea, with no rate for which to qualify. He knew that he would swab decks, paint, and cook for the next several months. He and how many others performed those menial tasks.

Gill removed his shoes and socks, put the letter in one of the shoes, and his billfold in the other. He gazed out across the vast darkness of the ocean, broken only by the reflection of lights from the ships, far out to sea, and from the buildings along the boardwalk. He rolled up his pants and stepped into the water.

The Pacific at San Diego is never warm. In fact, the current from Alaska always keeps the water cooler than most people enjoy. He waited a moment, then went a little deeper. Again, he waited, then waded deeper.

Suddenly, a voice out of the darkness behind him broke the ocean's trance, as he heard it say, "Mister, your shoes are going to wash away and you are going to get your uniform wet, if you go any further." Gill turned and saw the incoming tide washing closer to his shoes and saw the small body of a boy in the shadow of the beach. "Thanks!" he said, then turned and walked back toward the beach. He touched the boy on his head and said thanks again, as he picked up his shoes and started toward a bench.

"Thank you, Mister, for serving our country. My daddy is way out there on a ship, cooking for all of those men, and keeping the ship, me and mommy real safe."

Strange how God uses the voice of a child to change the heart and direction of a broken man. The tour of duty at sea was not perfect. He mopped a lot of decks but he made it. He did it and he served well.

May

Mothers and Memorials

Mom Had a Good Nose

When I was about ten, Johnnie Barber and I decided that we would smoke a cigar. We each purchased a large Tampa Nugget and went way down in back of my house behind my dad's work shop. We smoked those cigars as fast as we could. I mean, we did not waste a moment, we puffed, we pulled, we tried to blow smoke out of our noses and to blow smoke rings. Most of what we did was coughed and coughed and puffed and puffed. Long before the cigars were gone, we were gone.

Johnnie went to his house and me to my house. I was green, sick, dizzy, and in a state of death, for sure. The moment I ran in the house my mother said, "Sonny, you have been smoking." I didn't bother to answer. I just headed to the bathroom. Then to my room, feeling I was nearing the pearly gates. They didn't look too pearly, only looked smoky.

When the sickness finally left, I tried my best to figure out how mother knew. I was not smart enough to know that since no one in our family smoked, she could smell me coming up the back walk. But I always woke a bit cautious about my mother, for I just knew she had x-ray vision and mind-reading skills.

Johnnie survived the test of manhood. Life on Lindsey Street moved forward. By the way, God does have x-ray vision and mind-reading comes natural to Him.

Mad House

My three sisters, their children, and husbands all gathered on Christmas Eve. Dad handed out gifts. The madness would begin! Paper flew, ribbons sailed, and laughter filled the air.

I always loved Christmas: sounds, smells, green trees, colored lights, bright stars on top, gifts under the tree, the aroma of food cooking, laughter of children, marking the Sears and Roebuck catalogue, and turning down pages so 'Santa would know'. How could I live at 246 South Lindsey Street and not love Christmas?

We always depended on Mother to do something very funny. She opened one large box, pulled out a lamp shade, and pushed the box aside, which got filled up with paper. Later, Dad asked how she liked her lamp.

"What lamp?" she asked, "I got a lamp shade but didn't see any lamp." We all hurried to the back yard, and dug through the pile. There in the large box, with thrown away paper, was mother's lamp.

Another year, she prepared three dozen deviled eggs, which we found three days later in the refrigerator. We had a table so full, it almost fell under the weight of the food. More than anything, we had each other.

Mom and Dad spent fifty years throwing a party for all of us. Time finally ran out. The crowd did not gather, the children did not chatter, and the old table just looked alone and empty. It was wonderful while it was happening. I am forever the better for it.

God Does Not Have an Eraser

David walked down Bourbon Street and turned right onto St. Peter's. The air was pungent with odors of the night before. The fog from the Mississippi River kept the odors close to the ground.

David had never smelt such an odor. Street crews were washing off spilled beer from the night before, while others gathered trash, to throw in a truck. The whole area appeared to be suffering from a hangover from a night of riotous living.

David felt a breeze as he reached Jackson Square. At least here, the air was breathable. David saw her leaning against the front of St. Louis Cathedral. Her back against the building, her head hung way over. She was pitiful, covered in layers of clothing, no doubt wearing her entire wardrobe. Her skin, a color of death, with hair matted, she smelled of French Quarter streets.

David walked to the café, got two beignets, a large coffee, a couple of creamers, some sugar, and a stirring stick. He walked back to the woman. "Marie, how about a cup of coffee and beignet?" he asked. She stirred, pulled her head back against the cathedral wall and said, "How you know me? I ain't never seen you. I'm closed, no business today, go away."

"Here take the coffee," David said, holding it so the aroma filled the pungent air. "I'm not here for business, just time, how about this?" Then he placed a hundred dollar bill in her hand, watched as she wadded it up.

Marie placed it inside her blouse. She said, "You crazy man. Nothing I know is worth that much bread." After a sip of coffee and bite of beignet, she looked into his face.

"I just came to share a minute," David said. "I know what happened when you were fifteen. I know about your dad the preacher, the boyfriend, your dad took you to the abortion clinic in New York. I know all that, Marie. I wonder, do you remember a Sunday in July when you were nine; you were saved and then baptized? I was wondering."

"So long ago," Marie said. "I know by now God has wiped my name from His Book. I didn't mean to do that, we just got crazy one night and my world fell apart. Daddy went crazy. We killed that baby, I turned eighteen, and I left and never looked back. Who are you, how do you know all that? I must be crazy after all the years living in this hole!"

"You are not crazy, Mother," David said, "Just frightened, confused, and I have come to take you out of this hole. God does not erase what He writes in His Son's blood. You ready?" He held out his hand. Marie looked into his eyes and said, "What did you call me?"

"Marie," David answered.

Marie went on, "No, before that, you said, 'Mother'. Mother! I can't be a mother, I can't! I am not fit." "Time to go, Mom, time to go", as David took her hand. He looked and saw her worn out form lying now on the sidewalk of the Cathedral, "Let's go home, Mom, let's go home."

The Cost of Freedom

At Pointe du Hoc, 4:30 am on June 6, 1944, under command of Lt. Col. James Earl Rudder, there were 225 men in Second Ranger Battalion who made their way toward the point of land which separated Utah and Omaha beaches. These were the two primary beaches assaulted by American forces on D-Day. Due to high wind and seas, the Higgins boats were off course and delayed until the element of surprise was removed from the battle. Their mission was to scale the 100 foot cliffs, at ninety degrees straight up. On top of the cliffs were 300 Germans who manned six 155mm guns, which the Battalion had to put out of action. These guns had a range of 15 miles, which could strike both Omaha and Utah beaches, and strike ships bringing men to shore. The guns had to be put out of action.

The Higgins boats were armed with rocket launchers designed to fire grapple hooks to the top of the cliffs. Due to the water soaked condition of the ropes, many of the hooks failed to reach the top of the cliffs. The Battalion made their assault, climbed to the top, and took the Pointe.

When we visited Pointe du Hoc recently, a Frenchmen told about those 1944 Germans did not know what grapple hooks were. The Germans thought the grapples were some kind of bomb, did not pull the grapples loose, which allowed Rangers to reach the top.

On reaching their destination, the Rangers learned that five big German guns had been moved a mile inland to an apple orchard, in order to protect them from Navy shelling. The Rangers found the guns, and put all six out of commission. The battle was won.

However, relief did not come for the Second Battalion as planned on that day. By the time relief arrived on June 8, there were only 90 of 225 men left. Out of water and low on ammunition, Lt. Col. Rudder and his men held on to their position and saved countless American lives from German forces at the top of the Pointe.

Thank you, men of Second Battalion, and countless others, who did their best, and gave their all, that I might write this in a free country and send it across our world.

Forgotten

n this Memorial Day, our Nation will honor and remember Slim and thousands of our Veterans like him.

Slim 'Too Tall" Gray, as they called him back in Iraq, had lived for two years on the streets of Nashville. He hung around the mission for a few weeks. Then he ventured onto the streets, slept under bridges, in vacant buildings, and anywhere he could find a spot away from others. He ate at the mission and from food thrown away by area restaurants.

Slim's journey had started in Iraq, as he walked two feet behind and eight feet to the right of Johnson, his best friend. When Johnson stepped on a mine, the explosion not only took his life, but the burning debris of the mine burned Slim's face and burned Slim's clothing through to his left arm.

The Medic in Iraq, who came to his aid, told Slim that he found him weeping as he covered Johnson's body with his own. Since they were backed up with more seriously injured soldiers, who waited on the Medivac Team to take them to the field hospital, they put Slim in a jeep going to the same location.

A doctor at the field hospital decided that they could take care of Slim's burns and not send him out of country for treatment. In a couple of days, Slim helped out with other wounded soldiers. After about ten days, the hospital handed Slim a folder of papers to give to his Lieutenant and told him to catch the next chopper going to his unit.

One of the medical clerks told Slim to be sure to get the folder to the Lieutenant because his promotion to Corporal was in there, as well as his Purple Heart Award.

Slim gave the folder to his Lieutenant. Unknown to Slim, the Lieutenant put them in his personal bag of items and four days later, the Lieutenant was killed. Slim's papers went home to the officer's family.

Two months later, Slim's new Lieutenant realized that Slim "dug in" each time he heard an explosion. The Lieutenant decided, with eleven months of service in the combat zone, Slim should be sent home.

Discharged and back in Nashville, life was more like combat than home for Slim. His wife decided she had taken all she could. With divorce papers in hand, she took off to Texas.

Slim made one visit to the VA but his luck never changed. Slim picked a bad day for the clerk assigned to him. Slim was told he had no benefits and to go to work.

It was life on the streets of Nashville for Slim. He lasted another year and one Sunday morning, his body was found near the river. Burial was at the Middle Tennessee Veterans Cemetery in Pegram, with the headstone marked as PFC Clifton 'Slim' Gray. No family, no honor, just another casualty of a very long war.

The Wall

You know the 'Wall', the Vietnam Veterans Memorial, the great black wall that now displays the names of 58,318 men and women (as of Memorial Day 2017). The 'Wall' that holds the names of 154 men who received the Medal of Honor, the names of six sets of brothers and three pairs of fathers and sons, 8 female nurses, 16 Chaplains, one who received the Medal of Honor. I have visited the 'Wall' a number of times.

From our own Upper Cumberland area, S 4 Class James T. Davis is listed as the first man killed in a battlefield action. 997 men were killed on their first day in country and 1,443 died the day they were coming home. That is the 'Wall'.

Early in the morning, once young men, now old men will be at the 'Wall'. The same happens all day and into the dark of night, when the 'Wall' becomes as black as the night. Men who came home but left so much of themselves in that far off country, they have never returned, not really.

My nephew, Danny Ayers, is on that 'Wall'. I have his name on paper marked in black from where I rubbed it for his memory. Just a kid, life never got to him, he left it in that far off country.

With the troubles of our country, it helps my heart to think of all of those who paid so very much. In their living and dying, they still remind us that we have a great land.

Stand and look at that 'Wall'. That is who we really are, not the bitterness and disgruntles that fill our news today. Come on America, stand up, be your best. Put yourself into a position to see the dream, the dream that those 58,318 young men had in their eyes. See it reflected in that black 'Wall', that is who we are.

Vietnam Memorial – A Good Man

The 9 pm darkness of D.C. could not hide the eternal darkness of the Vietnam Memorial, with its more than 50,000 names inscribed on its black granite. Somehow the unlit, V-shaped memorial poked its sobering majesty through the darkness and into my heart. I had asked the park ranger, Victor Pillar, to look up two names for me to locate. One name was my nephew Sgt. Danny R. Ayers, killed September 14, 1968 at the age of 21. The other name was SP4 James Thomas Davis, from Livingston Tennessee, killed December 22, 1961, at the age of 24, becoming the first combat casualty of the Vietnam War.

The park ranger quickly found both of them. Then he told me that Davis was on the top of the highest plate on the memorial. He said I would need a ladder to reach the name and make a marker of the inscription. I thanked him for his concern and said that I would return in the morning.

I walked down the dark path and stood gazing at the darkness of all those men killed in the name of their Nation. While I have visited this sobering place before, it was always in the day time. It seemed to me that the darkness pushed the sadness of this honored ground deep into my soul. I stood there looking into the dark at all of those men, who gave their lives for our country. Until this memorial was built, it seemed to me that no one noticed and no one cared.

My eyes filled with tears as I thought of all of the families who had holes in their hearts because of their loss. Then suddenly, I saw the park ranger, Victor Pillar, ladder in one hand and a flashlight in the other, looking for me. He placed the ladder by the correct plate, climbed to the name, and holding the light in his mouth, made a marker of the inscribed name.

Almost in tears, I told him I did not know how to properly pay him. I only heard him say, "Sir, these men paid me a long time ago. It was my privilege to do this for them and for you." There may be a lot wrong in Washington, but there is also Victor Pillar. He is proof that there is good in our nation's capital.

A Broken Nation

My grandfather, Arthur Raley, was about six feet tall and his hair was white like snow. I asked my grandmother once why his hair was so white. She said, "Your grandfather is like Jesus. He is a really good man."

Years later as I read this passage, I realized where she got her answer. I smiled, knowing after all those years together, she could still call him a really, really good man.

Yesterday, I watched as person after person praised their mothers. I did the same in my message. My family had the joy of being the age when parents were right, and when they stuck it out through hard times. In spite of all the faults and failures, they still found the best in their partners.

My mother loved my dad all of those years and he returned that love. I am sure they had moments of conflict, yet never was a moment that not being together was in question.

Remember the rhyme from your childhood, "Humpty Dumpty"? "Humpty Dumpty sat on a wall; Humpty Dumpty had a great fall. All the king's horses and all the king's men could not put Humpty together again."

We have a broken nation. The pieces are scattered most in all of our families. Until we allow our Lord to put our families together again, our world will remain broken. Pieces that cannot be put together by "all the king's horses and all the king's men". Only God can put together a shattered nation. It will not start in Washington, D.C. It must start in our homes.

June

Fathers

What's a Dad?

Two police officers in car 197 received a silent alarm call from a warehouse rear door in one of the worst sections of town. They turned into the alley, stopped, and called for a backup to cover the front door.

When they were in place, they closed in on the back door. They thought they saw something move behind the trash dumpster. They placed all their lights on the dumpster, called out, "Police! Whoever's behind the dumpster, come out and show your hands!"

Nothing happened. They approached the dumpster from different sides with their weapons drawn. All they could see was a large piece of cardboard. One officer grabbed at it, while the other officer held his weapon and light on it. The figure of a small boy emerged, about seven, wrapped in a dirty blanket, trembling with fear.

The officers holstered their weapons. They pulled the child from underneath the cardboard. By now, he was crying, asking them not to hurt him.

One of the officers called for a female officer and social worker. The officers worked to assure him that he was not in trouble, and they had come to help him. When one officer asked where his dad was, the boy looking very confused asked, "What's a Dad?"

Could this be what's wrong with America? We are missing Dads.

His Sleeping Spot

John got to his doctor's appointment a few minutes early; this was not his first time here. In fact, this had come to seem like a regular stop on his journey of life these past four months.

John had seen several medical specialists, other doctors, and had uncountable tests run. Now he was going to sit and listen to his long time physician and friend wrap it all up for him.

The staff treated John like one of the family. They kidded and teased him about coming so much they were going to name a chair after him. Shirley, the doctor's nurse, called his name and led him back to the doctor's office, not an exam room, but the office. He had been Dr. Welch's patient for twenty years and long ago, they became good friends.

After the greeting, John said, "Well, what's the verdict, Doc? Give me the news." The doctor put his hand on his friends shoulder and said, "How much do you want to know, John?" "Everything, Doc, give me all of it." Then the darkness came and time seemed to stand at attention, not moving, just silence in the ticking of the clock.

The doctor explained that it was indeed cancer. In fact, by all of his experience and of all the specialists he had seen, there was little left for them to do other than make him comfortable. With their knowledge and past cases of this cancer, it was only a matter of time. Not very much of that either, maybe six months, maybe another month or two, either way at the most.

"I am sorry my friend," Dr. Welch said, "I sure have dreaded today and this conversation. We are too close for me to do otherwise than to tell you the entire story, John." John thanked him and they hugged. Then they talked of what he might expect and what they could do about his pain. Since he lived alone, what plans he needed to make, and with what choices the doctor could help him.

The doctor let him out of the door that led directly into the hall across from the elevators. John spoke to himself, inside his own soul, as he rode down the six stories and walked to his car. As he drove away he said, "Well, Lord, you heard all of that, and I am sure you already knew. I sure am glad that we are friends and that you are going to be here to walk with me these next several months. Help me, Lord, to know that you are here. Help me to try not to assign blame, not to be bitter, and to leave with the same great friendship we have had over these last forty years. Going to need to be a bit closer, Lord, but I know you won't mind. When it is time, Lord, just touch my hand, so that I will know to follow you." Four months and six days later, as John turned to find a sleeping spot in his bed, he felt 'His Hand'. When the nurse came the next morning to check on him, there he was in his sleeping spot.

With Dad

ad got me up real early and said that we were going to see something really great, but I would have to hurry.

Tom Stewart picked us up in the Compress car. We went down to this large lot that the Compress owned. Dad showed me two trains that were parked on the side tracks of the railroad. One train was full of people and the other train had animals. It was the Ringling Brothers Barnum and Baily Circus trains. They were going to Jackson for a one night show.

We watched as horses and elephants pulled Circus carts, loaded with supplies, down to the lot. The animals also helped men spread the heavy canvas and put up four tall posts, which would provide the main support of the great Circus tent.

The canvas was spread and the poles where in place. About 20 elephants surrounded the tent, each holding a rope leading to the center posts. On the command of the 'tent boss' they began to walk away from the canvas, holding the ropes. We stood there spell bound as the great 'Big Top' began to rise into the air.

Workers, like ants, moved over the lot. Soon, all was in place for the one night stand of the Greatest Show on Earth. This may have been one of their last small town, one night stands. It was a once-in-a-lifetime experience for me.

After we had finished gawking at the event, Dad suggested that we go up to South Royal Café and have breakfast. I think this was one of the very few times that we ate out when I was a child. He ordered me eggs, bacon, toast, and orange juice. We sat on the stools at the bar, having a great breakfast.

Of all the events of that morning, nothing was as wonderful as eating breakfast at the South Royal Café with my father. That was the event of the day.

See, Dad, it doesn't take a lot to impress your child. In fact, the most important thing it takes, is you.

Frozen Fish

When I taught school, I raised tropical fish in the class room. The children seemed to enjoy watching the fish. They also helped me feed the fish, and clean the fish tanks.

One Christmas, I purchased some small bowls, filled each with water, and gave each child two fish to take home for Christmas.

I told the children they could bring the fish back or they could keep the fish. The choice was theirs.

The first day back after the holidays, several children returned with fish and stories. They wanted to tell about their fish names and all that had happened. One pair of fish had reproduced. The bowl was now full of small fish. Another fish had jumped out of the bowl, landed in the kitchen sink, and lived a full day, before he was noticed in the sink. Most of the children wanted me to see that they had cared for their fish and enjoyed getting the fish back to our large Aquariums.

Bobby said that his fish had died. I told him I was very sorry but that sometimes when you change fish water, they will catch something and not live very long.

Bobby said, "Mine froze to death." I explained how these fish should have been kept in the house, with a lamp over the bowl. We had talked about this before they left for the holidays.

Bobby looked at me with those big eyes and said, "Mr. Raley, I could only keep my fish in my room. They froze. The water froze solid."

I said I understood. I told him when summer came, he could have some more fish, to put in a pan out in the yard, in sunlight to keep them nice and warm. The day ended and I kept thinking about what Bobby had said, 'They froze solid in my room.'

On my way home that evening, I drove by Bobby's house. As I entered the smoke filled room, my eyes stung from a bucket of coal burning in the middle of the floor. The family was huddled around that bucket, bodies covered with blankets, eating dinner out of paper plates. The children were excited but the parents were embarrassed. We visited. I asked if they could use a stove, if I could find one.

The father said they didn't want to be a burden, but with no vent for the fire, he had to let it go out at night, due to harmful fumes. The house got very cold, with weather in the 20's. I called a man who owned a furniture store, and told their story. The next day Bobby and his family had a new stove with a vent. Everyone was warm the first time since summer.

I am thankful that Bobby, now a middle aged parent, lives in a house with central heat and air. His family can raise all the tropical fish they desire. He is a great father, soon to be grandfather, and he has come a long way from a bucket of coal in his living room. Maybe that frozen fish was a message from the Lord.

I am thankful for a frozen fish. What are you thankful for?

Someone to Care

As I visited the hospital one day, I stopped and spoke to the 'Pink Lady', who has often helped me when I was trying to locate a patient.

The 'Pink Lady' mentioned that they had a new magazine in the lobby with a story about my dad, which I had written. She went and got the magazine, turned to the story and said, "Wait here just a minute." Then the 'Pink Lady' walked over to an older lady, sitting with a young lady who looked like an adult grandchild.

The older lady pointed to the story, then to me. In a few minutes, the older lady asked if I would join them. I walked over and introduced myself and sat in the chair across from her and her granddaughter. The older lady pointed to the story and told me she would be doing a lot of that in the next several days.

The story was about a man coming to pay his respects to my dad in the funeral home at Jackson. I asked the older lady what had happened. She said that her husband had just died. They were waiting for their pastor and some family members. The older lady and her granddaughter had been in the chapel, but they were afraid that it would be hard to be found. The two ladies had come out to the main lobby where they could be seen.

After I expressed my regrets, I offered to pray with her, which she seemed pleased. Then she was very grateful that I waited until the family began to gather.

I returned to the 'Pink Lady' volunteer and expressed my appreciation for her care and gentile behavior, way above the line of duty. She smiled and said, "It is always good to be someone who cares."

As I drove home, I wondered how many people the 'Pink Lady' had touched and blessed with her gentle spirit of Christ. Everyone needs someone who cares.

Words of the Wise

"The words of wise men are heard in quiet more than the cry of him that ruleth among fools." Ecclesiastes 9:17 (KJV)

ot traveling to class, but the turning of pages left him wise.

Sometimes I think you could put all the words that my father spoke in a gallon jug. He was quiet. Yet when you reached into him, you realized that silence was not the absence of knowledge, but in fact the presence of wisdom.

My father did not have a lot of the formal education that most of us enjoy today. His stopped at the twelfth grade, which for his generation was considered very adequate. The absence of education had nothing to do with the volume of wisdom that he possessed.

Dad's was a cup that overflowed. Some of my best memories are etched in seeing him read. It seemed to me that he read everything that had writing on it. What he did not receive in the halls of education, he more than made up for in the pages of the volumes he read.

Slow to speak, but filled with the wisdom that made each day rich. If I could change a quality of my life, it would be that I was quieter, less quick to speak, and more like my dad.

We Were There

enior citizens were there on that 'Longest Day' in the Battle at Normandy. When more than 100,000 men swarmed the beaches of Normandy, France, one outstanding citizen is listed high among them. Brigadier General Theodore Roosevelt, Jr., at fifty-seven years of age, was the only general in the Allied forces to make the landing on the first wave that rainy morning on June 6, 1944.

As Assistant Division Commander of the 4th Infantry Division, 1st Army, the Big Red One, General Roosevelt led his men to the Utah Beach landing, riding in a Higgins Boat, as thousands of other American troops landed.

Because of a navigational error, the landing took place in the wrong inlet. Realizing this, Roosevelt understood that his officers and men were confused. Their maps were unusable. He took charge of the invasion, ordered the remaining troops to land in the same inlet. He led his men over the sea wall, cleared the beachhead, and outflanked the Germans. Roosevelt was able to link up with the Airborne Division that had landed inland in the early morning hours of the battle. The Army not only recognizes him as the highest ranking officer to make the first wave, but also the oldest American on the beach for the landing.

Brigadier General Roosevelt, son of the late United States President Teddy Roosevelt, had served in the First World War along with two of his brothers. His brother, Quentin Roosevelt was killed in France in an air battle of that war.

Before making the landing at Normandy, Brigadier General Roosevelt had served in North Africa, Sicily, and Italy, receiving the Silver Star and other commendations for his service in those battles.

Roosevelt was the oldest, highest ranking officer, and was also the only father with a son who made the same landing. Theodore Jr's son, Quentin Roosevelt II, was named for Theodore's fallen brother, and was also in the D-Day invasion.

Fans of the movie, 'The Longest Day', remember that Henry Fonda portrayed General Roosevelt. Roosevelt walked with a cane due to arthritis. In spite of all his drawbacks, this senior citizen did a great service by rising above and beyond the call of duty for his nation, himself, his deceased father, and all of us old guys. He was also awarded the Medal of Honor for his bravery at Normandy.

Part of the orders for the Medal of Honor: "After two verbal requests to accompany leading assault elements in the Normandy invasion had been denied, Brig. Gen. Roosevelt's written request for this mission was approved. He landed with the first wave of forces assaulting enemy-held beaches. He repeatedly led groups from the beach, over the seawall, and established them inland.

His valor, courage, and presence at the very front of the attack and his complete unconcern for his own safety, being under heavy fire, inspired the troops to heights of enthusiasm and self-sacrifice.

Although the enemy had the beach under constant direct fire, Brig. Gen. Roosevelt moved from one locality to another, rallying men around him, directed and personally led them against the enemy. Under his seasoned, precise, calm, and unfaltering leadership, assault troops reduced beach strong points and rapidly moved inland with minimum casualties. He thus contributed substantially to the successful establishment of the beachhead in France."

General Omar Bradley, Commander of the 1st Army, said of Roosevelt's bravery, "It was the single bravest act that I witnessed in the entire war." Had it not been for Roosevelt's bravery and leadership, most of his division would have been killed in the confusion of the early moments of the battle.

Brigadier General Theodore Roosevelt, Jr. died in France on July 12, 1944 from a heart attack, two days before receiving the message from Headquarters of his promotion to Major General and being given Command of his own division.

Roosevelt is buried in the American Cemetery at Normandy next to his brother, Quentin, whose body was moved from a WWI burial ground to be next to his brother, Theodore Roosevelt, Jr.

As I stood before those graves in France, I thanked our Lord for brave men and women who gave their all for our country. Someone might be interested to know that the two Theodore Roosevelt's are one of only two sets of Father and Sons, to be awarded the nation's highest honor. The other father-and-son team being the Macarthur's.

I stood at Roosevelt, Jr's grave and gave thanks to our Heavenly Father for the faithfulness of this man, who did not have to make this journey but who fought to do so because he loved his country.

Before victory came, we left more than 200,000 young men in Europe. Homes across America would be empty, and hearts would be broken, but you and I would remain free.

Father, we pause to give thanks for these and so many others, even to this very day, that have paid such a great price for our privilege of being free. The debt can only be paid by our being faithful men and women. Forgive us our sin and direct us by Your Light.

July

Freedoms

America, My Home

What is it that makes America great? I am sure that you could get a lot of answers by asking a lot of different people. We all have our niche, that special portion of this wonderful country that makes it great in our hearts.

We certainly had a great beginning. Our founding fathers took huge risks and many of them paid with all of their wealth, as well as their lives. They found themselves out numbered and out gunned, yet they won. They put their faces in the dirt and prayed that God would give His shining approval to their work and their dreams.

We certainly had great tests along the way. No one had tried a democracy like ours and those early years found us struggling. Through it all and in spite of our enemies, we prevailed. We fought within ourselves and watched more than a half of a million of our men die. We struggled to overcome the disaster. Somehow both sides lifted their hearts in prayer for their cause and God allowed His just cause to be victorious.

We defended our friends in great wars, watched our young men die, and put every American to work to win battles against evil.

We walked on the moon, and went to the bottom of the sea. We climbed our economy until it was the great oak tree, standing in the middle of the forest of nations, showing others what it was like to be built on free enterprise.

We have before us our greatest challenge. Can we recover our character, and remember our foundation? Can we return to our values, and realize the blessing of our Heavenly Father, the founder and Creator of life, liberty, and the pursuit of happiness?

Tomorrow will be greater than today. The past will form our future. The future will be greater than our hearts dreams if we will but put our faces in the dust and call upon our founder to return us to our beginning and bless us once again.

The greatest task will be to begin on our knees and to humbly seek His face. America, my home sweet home.

When Life Was Simple

ife was simple when I was a boy at 246 South Lindsey Street. In the winter, we went to school, then 'played out' till dark, as we called it in the yard, if it was not too cold. Then we had supper, listened to the radio and went to bed.

In the summer, we just spent the day outside. Sure we had chores. Those were going to the grocery store, about three blocks away, cutting the yard, feeding the pets and a few other things as mother remembered to ask me to do. For the most part, we played out.

Johnnie Barber and I were next door neighbors. Most of the time, we formed a group of boys and girls involved in cowboys and Indians, baseball, building a fort out of sticks and old lumber on the vacant lot, and just hanging around.

We rode sticks for horses and held other sticks for guns. In general, we pretended that so many things were real. I collected leaves from trees, put them in a bag and called it money. We chipped the concrete off bricks, and had a great pile of them, with which later my father would brick our house. We called it gold.

In later years, we road our bikes, and cut other people's yards for about 25 cents. We went to the store for anyone who would let us, and most often they gave us a nickel. We wondered what girls were all about. It was simple, fun, safe, and we looked forward to each new day.

I remember Betty Upton teasing me because I had only a plain stick for my horse. She assured me that I did not know which way I was going, forward or backward. I fixed her. I stuck one end of my stick horse in a can of white paint and called it the head. That way, I always knew which way I was going.

Betty was the one thing or person that Johnnie and I disagreed on. We both 'claimed' her, strange language, but that is what we called it in those days. This sometimes caused a falling out in our friendship but for never more than a few hours. After all, a girl couldn't come between us guys.

We listened to the Lone Ranger, Sky King, and Gang Busters on the radio and replayed them in the yards and fields of Lindsey Street.

Life was simple, innocent, and good. In my old age, I sometimes dream at night of that street, those kids, and the joys of having very little, but feeling very fortunate.

Life is not simple now. It is not innocent. The dreams of a boy are now brief, fuzzy, and not so many as long ago.

A Word from Ben

Americans need to hear once more from Ben Franklin:

"To our founding fathers in the dawn of the birth of our nation. In the beginning of the Contest with Great Britain, when we were sensible of danger we had daily prayers in this room for the divine protection.

Our prayers, Sir, were heard, & they were graciously answered. All of us, who were engaged in the struggle, must have observed frequent instances of a superintending providence in our favor.

I have lived, Sir, a long time, and the longer I live, the more convincing proofs I see of this truth, that God governs in the affairs of men. And if a sparrow cannot fall to the ground without his notice, is it probable that an empire can rise without his aid?"

Speaking of the writing of the Constitution:

"To that kind providence, we owe this happy opportunity of consulting in peace on the means of establishing our future national felicity. And have we now forgotten that powerful friend? Or do we imagine that we no longer need His assistance? We have been assured, Sir, in the sacred writings that 'except the Lord build the House, they labor in vain that build it'. I firmly believe this, and I also believe that without His concurring aid, we shall succeed in this political building no better than the Builders of Babel."

From me: The events of recent days remind us of the danger of leaving God out of our national dealings. Let each of us, on our knees before God, thank Him for the answer He gave to our founding fathers. Let us humbly beseech Him to hear our prayer of confession, our desire for forgiveness, and our call for His help, in our moving forward as a great nation. Not for our greatness but that in our strength, others might be strengthened, and through our power, others might enjoy the fruit of freedom and faith in God.

The Silent Greatest Generation

All of us love to pay tribute and give honor to the more than 16 million men and 640,000 women who served in our armed services in the Second World War. Almost half a million men never came home, and we call them members of the 'Greatest Generation'.

Certainly we should call them Greatest, for their sacrifices purchased freedom for us from those who would have destroyed our very way of life.

However, somehow we have forgotten that remaining portion of the greatest generation. We have forgotten those who stayed on the home front and who furnished our men and women everything they needed to win victory.

By the day after Pearl Harbor, Americans moved toward 'war awareness'. All were called upon to save items used to build materials needed for victory. Farmers worked twice as hard to raise food. Even children gathered tin cans for the 'victory drive'.

Before the war came to a finish, almost 90% of single women and 80% of married women had worked in some way for victory. Six million women, who had never worked outside the home, took those skills and learned new ones which kept our 'boys' supplied. "Rosie the Riveter" was joined by millions.

In that short time, they built 564 Destroyer Escorts, 387 Destroyers, 87 Cruisers, 9 Battleships, 151 Air Craft Carriers, 126 Submarines and 2,751 Liberty Ships. They also built 100,000 aircraft and 100,000 tanks, plus millions and millions of ammunition rounds. No other nation in the entire world has ever achieved such goals. To put it in a different light, neither Germany nor Japan built even one ship during that time. They never replaced a ship that we sunk at the Battle of Midway.

Hitler accused his generals of lying to him when they told him they had shot down 40 Allied planes in one night. The next night, we had just as many over Germany. His generals told him that each time they shot down one plane, we built two more.

Stand up 'Working People' of America, take a bow, and join your rightful place in 'The Greatest Generation.'

Watching Bottles

*T*he family lived down by the railroad tracks. You might even say they lived on the wrong side of the tracks. They kept a neat little house. In the summer, you always found them on the front porch, waving at all who went by their home.

A lot of people pitied them. They seemed so poor and so unprepared for this fast paced world that had started at the end of the WWII. He had worked for the local Coke bottler, watching bottles as they came out of the washer, and pulling those that were not clean off the line. Thus, his job seemed to be so boring and unimportant - to many.

I used to stop by and spend some time on their front porch on my way home from the popcorn stand where I worked. They were great listeners. I was always filled with questions. I loved to hear him talk about his days in Europe as a member of the Army, from 1942 to 1945.

He never talked about himself. It was about the men with whom he had served, and where he spent most of his time driving a truck. After D-Day, he had driven all the way to Germany with supplies and materials that men needed who were on the front line.

When he died, I went to his grave side funeral. I watched them fold the flag, and fire the guns. Then an officer presented the flag to his wife and opened a small box. The officer said, "With great honor to his wife, here is a Silver Star which he earned in battle in 1944.

It was never presented to him, but upon the authority of the President of the United States, I have been sent to give this medal to you on behalf of a grateful nation."

As the officer read the citation, he told how the soldier had stopped his truck, manned a machine gun, and held off the enemy while some thirty men loaded in his truck. He then took them to safety.

The Veteran had never mentioned that moment. He had talked about others who were brave but he had never told of the thirty men who had a chance to come home because he did more than was required.

Everyone thought he just looked at empty bottles. I just imagine in Glory, he met a lot of grateful and successful men because he did his best.

Operation Overlord at Normandy

Many remember the greatest invasion in the history of man, "Operation Overlord".

Over 160,000 young men, supported by 13,000 planes and 5,000 ships, left behind more than 9,387 graves at Normandy's Cemetery. An additional list of 1,557 names are those forever Missing In Action.

As I stood there one day, my tears were placed on that beautiful green grass as I prayed and thanked our Lord for those who gave so very much.

There are moments that hang like great drops of time in our memory. Such a moment was a Thursday, when I stood and looked across the American Cemetery and the beach at Normandy.

Lt. Murray Evans was a young man from Lindsey Street, who lived across the street from my family. He was in the first charge in that first wave up the beach on June 6, 1944. Lt. Evans led a group of young American teens into the land of France. For most of them, it became the Land of Eternity.

Lt. Evan's parents were wonderful friends of my family. I spent many hours on their front porch listening to the father, Mr. Evans. His 'boy' Murray is still on that beach in Normandy, along with more than 10,000 other young Americans. Lt. Evans was killed on the third day of that great battle. His family chose to allow his body to rest on that green grass of American soil.

As I stood before eight graves marked with the name unknown, I wept at those graves, saluted as an old man does, and then knelt in the dew covered grass. I thanked God for this 'unknown soldier' who paid with all he had. The unknown gave it all, so that over 68 years later, I stood before his marker and thanked him for those moments. When they charged that Normandy beach, they won another moment of freedom for the world.

Murray's parents were good, honest people, who deserved to have their son watch them grow old. The parents, of more than 400,000 other young men, were charged with their lives for our freedom, the same price of Murray's life.

As I looked across that beach, in my mind's eye, I saw Mary Lou Graft, wading ashore on the third day, as a nurse with the first Hospital Division. Those nurses established hope for those who were wounded. Mary Lou walked from the beach of Normandy, to the capital of the Nazi Empire in Berlin, to provide care for our American troops. She often spoke to me of those days.

Those memories were when she saw an enslaved world become free, because so many were willing to give their all.

That bubble of time held me captured, as I shed my tears for all the fallen, broken, and hopeful of those days. Thank you to all who crawled up that sandy, rock-covered beach, to unlock the door of liberty for me and others.

Our Broken World

We have known for a long time that something was wrong. We watched as our men came home from Vietnam, when no one cheered, and no one seemed to care. When my nephew, Danny, was killed in 'Nam, the article in the paper was so small, it was hard to find.

As I stood on the tarmac in Memphis waiting for his body, it was like I was waiting for freight. As I wept, it was so very sad for me to see that flag draped coffin. I looked around at those who were doing the unloading, as if it were just another package of freight. It broke my heart.

America had changed. We had become numb to the deaths of our men, weary of war, and forgetful of freedom. We mocked those who gave their all. We decided that the world owed all of us something. We were each going to claim it, without the responsibility of paying the price of liberty and freedom. Let someone else do the job.

When our twin towers fell, we revived for a few months. We almost returned, we heard the call of danger, and we saw the suffering that a few could cause. Soon, our churches were empty again, and our prayers were more for the market, than for the plan and purpose of God.

On a Friday night, when her people suffered, France joined us. Her great city fell victim to a few, who believed that nothing counts, just their will, and their wishes.

God still stands before the world and calls for our attention. He calls for us to receive His love, discover His will, live His way, and become a light so that others can find Him.

Maybe someone will notice this week. Maybe some life will change, some heart will listen, and someone will pray and obey.

Our broken world can only be put together by the plan and love of Christ. He alone holds the healing of the Nations, will you listen?

The Summer with Pepsi

*I*n the summer of 1994, the first time I met Augustus Bizimongu, he was wearing a shirt with a Pepsi logo on both the front and back. The last time I saw him he had on that same shirt, as he had on all the days that we were in Goma. Thus the nickname, 'Pepsi' seemed like a good choice, since I could not pronounce most of his real name.

Pepsi was about 19. While neither of us could speak the language of the other, we quickly learned how to communicate by either drawing in the black sand of the volcano, using sign language, or eye contact. It really worked well for both of us.

I knew very quickly that he was a leader. I gave Pepsi a task and it got done. I placed him in charge of a team of twelve men, who dug a large latrine for five hundred people, who would live on our camp sight.

At the days end, he came out of that ditch. He climbed wearily up the ladder from a ten foot deep hole, covered in the black dust of volcanic ash that was to be home to our five hundred people.

Pepsi came back the next day, ready to get back in the hole, and finish the task. Somewhere, somehow, he had washed his Pepsi shirt and again he wore it. The story repeated itself for the weeks it took to dig the large hole. Never a complaint, and always a smile. With a motion from me for a great days work from him, he came back in the morning sunlight.

As we completed the camp, we began to make our preparations to return to the U. S. With sadness in his eyes, I took his picture, and gave a copy to all those locals who were in charge of jobs. I assured them that he was a great worker.

On the last day in camp, I hid all the clothes I did not need, in order to get home. I told Pepsi where they were and that they were his, after I left. We said our goodbyes to all of the men.

As our truck turned to leave, Pepsi ran in front and stopped us. Pepsi gave me a small brass cup, and I gave him a pen, which was the last thing I had that I could spare. Tears ran down both of our faces, knowing we would never see one another again, in this life. I put my thumb in the air, 'well done' was the sign. Well done.

I never received any information about him but have wondered many times if he found a job, a wife, and a new life. The Mt. Nyiragongo eruption destroyed the camp in 2002 and much of the city of Goma. Some 500,000 people were left homeless. I hope he was safe. Pepsi had suffered so many dark nights. I hope that one missed him.

In our church service yesterday, I took the Lord's Supper from that cup which Pepsi gave me some 21 years ago. Pepsi, thanks for the summer of '94, thanks for the friendship, hard work, and a job well done.

See you in Glory. Thumbs Up!

August

Summertime

Visit Your Garden

"But the fruit of the Spirit is love, joy, peace, longsuffering, kindness, goodness, faithfulness, gentleness, self-control." Galatians 5:22, 23 (NKJV)

Each morning before the rest of us were awake, my grandmother would go to her garden, next door to their home on Tucker Street in Dyersburg, to choose some special items for the day. We would enjoy sliced tomatoes at breakfast, vegetables at lunch, and still other garden items at "supper" in the late afternoon. Sometimes there would be watermelon, or cantaloupes, and always beans and potatoes. All summer long, she would make that journey. She brought her basket filled with goodies back to the kitchen. The fruit of her garden for the table of her family.

Today, as we open a new work week, how about going into our garden of life and see how many of the fruits of the Spirit we have to harvest this week. Look at your wonderful gifts and choose some of them to bless others, as you move through the week.

Our country is weary of all the election news. What if we as Christians share our gifts and offer something better than what we are pelted with all day long? Share a smile, a prayer, a joy, give a thank you and let others see Jesus in you. I hope it will be as tasty as my grandmother's garden.

On The Porch

While my parents may have disliked what I had done, had been disappointed in my actions, or hurt by my decisions, I always knew that they would always love me and long to see me.

When I lived in Waynesboro, Tennessee, I would call home and let mother know that I was coming to visit them in Jackson. Mother said when she told Dad I was coming; he would go on our porch at 246 South Lindsey Street, sit in the swing and wait for me to come home.

Mother said, "Pop, you know how Ivan is. It might be three or four hours before he gets here. He might not leave on time or might stop a dozen times. You don't need to sit out here and wait on him." Dad said, "I know, but I would just like to be here when he turns off of Lexington Street onto Lindsey. I would just like to see him coming down the street."

Mother often said, "Well, Dad, you could have a lot done by the time he gets here." But Dad would just smile and say "I would just like to see him turning down the street."

When I made the turn from Lexington onto Lindsey, I saw him way down the street sitting on the porch at 246 South Lindsey, looking my way, waiting for me to come home.

Jesus must be that way about us. There in glory, He looks down the long road of time and I believe He will wait for Ivan to come home and greet him."

Your Investment

As Kyle left his townhouse, he decided to walk the blocks around his new 'billet'. He had spent 36 years in the Navy. Now at the age of 55, he was on his own and without a job, for the first time since he was 19.

Kyle had never married, lived most of his life in the quarters provided by the Navy and as a mustang Commander, he had lived in the Bachelor Officer's Quarters. Both at home and around the world, the years at sea and on Navy bases had given him an opportunity to meet a lot of people but he had only made surface friends.

His only family, a brother, lived more than two thousand miles away. He had not seen his brother in ten years or more, so all of this 'liberty' was new to him. He had chosen Buford, SC, as his retirement home because of the Navy bases and hospital, so even this area was a stranger to him.

His retirement was great; money was of no concern, but time. Time was a problem. No morning muster to check, no routine to follow. Any daily drills and schedules left his life an empty vessel.

As he circled the neighborhood, he discovered several open lots, almost like parks, but there was nothing there, just empty vacant space. The children he saw played in their yards, and the yards certainly seemed far too small to do any real playing.

There was a school in the area; it seemed to be for the younger grades. He knew that a number of children lived in the area. Where were the children when school was out and the school was closed?

After reading about the area and checking with the local parks department, he learned that the lots had been left by the developers of the subdivision. The lots were to be used as public property for parks of some sort. There had never been enough money to do anything more than keep them clean and mowed.

Kyle reached out to the families in the community. After a number of meetings and a lot of discussion, he began to develop one of the areas as a small softball field, along with playground equipment for younger children.

He discovered a couple of guys, with whom he had served and they lived in the area. With their help, the project was completed. Money was raised for a summer team of college students to oversee the park and keep it open for children all summer long.

Kyle would sit for hours on a bench and watch the children and their families play. He marveled at the joy they shared. He found his heart filled with his one quiet joy, for having found a project and bringing it to completion.

Is it not amazing how just regular people can make such a difference in the lives of others, when they decide to invest in the needs of someone beside themselves?

You don't have to build a park. You might just visit a lonely person or write a note to a hurting heart. Try it.

You Help Me and I Will Learn

One afternoon, I met the boys as they were playing basketball on a goal in my back yard. We talked a bit. I told them if they would come to church on Sunday morning, we would have a team and play Monday night.

The boys wanted to know if they could get uniforms. I went to the store, purchased shorts for all of them, and then got some matching shirts.

Next, I ironed their player numbers on the front and back. I let them choose their own numbers. To the boys, it was like getting a new car. Man, they were happy and I was in Heaven.

The boys really took to coming to church. They even came on Wednesday night. There they were on the front row, looking at me as if to say, "Here we are! Tell us something." The first time they attended on Prayer Meeting Night, I asked for prayer requests. Then I called on one of my men, Jack, to lead in prayer.

Before elder Jack could start praying, a boy on the front row named Jack looked up at me with fear but also determination in his eyes and said, 'I don't know how to do that but if you will help me, then I will learn.'

That was one of those Heaven on Earth moments. I smiled and explained to Jack that there was someone else in the room with his name. It was that man that I was asking to pray but I told him how proud I was of his willingness. I told him to listen as the 'other' Jack prayed and he would begin to learn.

After our older Mr. Jack got through with his prayer, we got through wading in the water, provided by all of our tears because of the bravery, innocence, and desire of our 'new' Jack. I explained to him how great a kid he was and how I knew that God had sent him into that room to teach all of us how to pray.

That was a moment you let God write in your heart and when you are old, it pops to the top and becomes a joy of life that makes a dull day sweeter.

Serving Others

As I pulled into the parking lot of Publix Food Market in Bellevue, TN, I found a great parking spot and started across the parking area to enter the store. A white haired man passed me, talking to himself. I related with him because I do a lot of that myself. I could tell that this was distressed talk, not happy.

I spoke to him and asked if it had been a bad day. He responded with, "The worst! I have been in the store for fifteen minutes and I cannot find one thing my wife put on this list."

As I laughed, I said something like, "Join the club. It happens to me all the time, but I have found a great solution." He looked interested, stopped his walking and said, "Share it with me."

We returned to the store. I spoke to one of the nice clerks and told her that my friend needed some help. She stopped what she was doing and asked how she could assist us. I handed her his list and told her that he could not find a thing in the store on that list.

She took one look, smiled at me, and said, "I can solve this." With that, she grabbed a buggy and asked him to follow her.

As I got what I wanted, I watched as he and the clerk returned to the front with a number of items. She showed him how to use the self-check-out and he loved watching it work.

He thanked the young lady, offered her a tip but she refused. I joined him as we walked out of the store and back to our cars.

He said, "Man, that reminds me of going to the store for my mom when I was a boy." "Right," I said, "They really know how to help a fellow here."

"You got that right," he said. "My wife is really going to be surprised. I have never finished one of her lists before."

We both laughed and parted ways.

I know nothing about the store or its national policy, but I know that at this store, they have a winning system.

Thank God for people who still like to serve others!

Wealth

hile I served as their pastor, I enjoyed visits to the King family home. Most visits were more for me than for them. I listened and learned while enjoying their company. The house was so small. I think it was a prefab home that had been placed by the large farm owner for them to live there. It might have been 1,200 sq. ft., with three very small bedrooms, a living room, eat-in kitchen, one bath and a large back porch for their family of five.

We spent most of our visits on that back porch, shared with three children, two dogs, and a pet goat. When we shared a meal, we served our plates in the kitchen, then headed to the porch to eat, fighting with the dogs and goat for our lunch.

In my memory, it was very funny. The family talked to the dogs and goat, like they understood every word. In truth, I think they did. Once you got to know the love they shared, the dreams they had, and the warm feelings for each other, it was very much a part of our time together. They were such humble people, and most would have called them poor. Humble, but not poor.

The King family taught what it is to really love one another and to allow that love to show in their lives. They never expressed any ill feelings toward the very wealthy man, who owned the house, and for whom they worked. They never had a bad word for others in our church family, who had great homes, wonderful clothes, beautiful cars, and large bank accounts.

Each day the King family got up with the joy of a task to be done, miles to travel, and dreams to see come true. Whenever I left their home, they always asked me to stay a bit longer. Before I left each time, they asked me to thank God for all that they had. I always left with tears in my eyes for a family who had so little, but enjoyed so very much.

The King family parents have gone to a really neat home in Glory. Their three children married people they loved, and live thankful, beautiful lives. I am so grateful that I met some really wealthy people in my journey through life. The Kings were near the top of the list.

Way to Go, Jennie

ou found Bill there each day, from 9 am to 6 pm, as he held Jennie's hand and sat by her bedside. It never varied much when he was there. It had been more than six months since she had said anything. He stayed, held her hand, and talked with her, just as if she understood every word he said.

Now and then, I dropped by the room at the nursing home, when we talked a few minutes. He always said, "Honey, the Pastor is here." Then he looked at me and said, "I am not sure, Pastor, if she hears well. I don't want her not to know who is in the room, since she never opens her eyes. I am not sure she can see anything."

As I sat with him a few minutes, we talked about the weather, news, and anything I brought up. Then I always prayed, kissed his wife on the forehead, and left with a handshake and a smile for him.

After almost a year of this long journey, Jennie died and I held her funeral. The church family shared their love and took care of him. He continued to attend church, and take part in the events of the community. Now his journey was not so direct. The smile, that had been his trademark, seemed to come only now and then.

One day, as he was leaving church after the service, he said, "Pastor, I saw Jennie last night. She said for me to thank you for your visits and for kissing her on her head. She told me to apologize for her never speaking back but the words would only form in her mind."

As I held his hand and hugged him a bit, there in the doorway of our church, I wasn't sure how else to respond. Then he looked up and said, "Pastor, Jennie thanked me for all those days of holding her hand and talking to her, even when she couldn't talk back."

Then in tears, he said, "Then Jennie said, 'I miss you honey but I sure do feel a lot better here. They are having a hard time keeping me from talking all the time'."

Bill hugged me back, turned and walked out the door. I simply smiled, looked up to Heaven and said, "Way to go Jennie, way to go."

September

School Days

How is Your Aroma?

"And walk in love, as Christ also has loved us and gave Himself for us, an offering and a sacrifice to God for a sweet-smelling aroma."
Ephesians 5:2 (NKJV)

How do you smell to God? Strange question yet appropriate. When a father hugs his son after a hard-fought football game, he doesn't smell the locker room odor, but rather the aroma of a well-played game, a battle on the field in which his son did his best.

God's word says, "Walk in my love and I will be pleased with the aroma."

The first thing that hit me when I walked from the airplane into the airport terminal was a thousand unsold, unused deodorant bottles. It did not get better when I hugged my friend, Jim Allen, as he waited for me after going through customs.

The aroma stayed with me during the hour long ride to the school. As the week progressed, homes were visited, classes were taught, games were played, and sermons preached. Also, heads were buried in my chest as people poured out their hearts, as they gave their lives to Christ. I forgot all about the unsold, unused packages of deodorant.

Three weeks later, as I walked into the terminal for my flight home, the strong pungent odor of my first entrance was gone. Now it was the hearts of those who came to see me leave, the tears shared, and the hugs of brothers in Christ.

There was Jim, with a lifetime of service to our Lord. Marko, the nine year old, who had adopted me as his American father, and "Big Footsball", the leader of the soccer team. Not only could God smell the aroma of changed lives, but my large nose picked up each of the drops of the long days, hot nights, and lives beginning again.

Thanks, Lord, for the new nose.

Do You Have A Coat Hanger?

The judge called and asked if there was any way that The Baptist Children's Home could find room that day for a family of three girls and two boys. He explained the father had been killed a couple of years earlier. The mother was on trial that day for her third DUI and she was going to jail. If the judge placed the children in state custody, he could not assure that the family would be kept together. He strongly believed in this case it was important to all of them to remain in contact.

I assured the judge that we would make it happen. One of our social workers and I went to a Pastor's office where the judge had arranged for the children to be kept temporarily. As the social worker interviewed each child, I tried to keep the others entertained. I tried to assure them, as terrible as it seemed, I believed they would discover it was not as bad as their fears.

I asked if they had any questions they wanted to ask me. The smallest boy wanted to know if we had any coat hangers. Now I expected to be asked about TV's, computers, ball equipment and a hundred other things, but never a coat hanger. So I said, "I am not sure I understood you, can you ask that again?" Once again, he asked if we had any coat hangers.

I asked him why a coat hanger was important. The boy said, "I have always wanted a coat hanger. When I go to my friend's house, his mother takes my coat and puts it on a coat hanger and then hangs it in a special place. At my house, we just throw our coats in the floor. Sometimes I use mine for cover, so I would like my own coat hanger.

I smiled, hugged him and said, "Son, you have died and gone to coat-hanger-heaven, for we have hundreds of coat hangers. I will be sure that you have several of your own, as well as a closet to hang them in." He smiled, rubbed back the tears, and hugged my neck.

Most of us have such long lists of our wants. Here was a small boy being taken from his home, and all he asked for was a coat hanger. "and a little child shall lead them*" and this boy did exactly that.

*(Isaiah 11:6 NKJV)

A Night on Interstate 40

en had walked about as long as his seventy year old legs would take him. The rain was beginning to pick up. The traffic along Interstate 40 still going the usual 80 mph, and was farther and farther apart. There was not much of a chance for anyone to stop in the rain at two o'clock in the morning.

He saw a road crossing just ahead and decided to try to find a dry spot under the bridge to keep him for the night. Near the top, where the crossover road met the dirt, was a nice level place out of the wind and rain. Ben bundled down for the night, and covered himself with a garbage bag he'd taken at the rest stop a few miles back.

Old Josh, as everyone called the dog, was barely moving down the side of the interstate. Rain still falling, his paws hurt, and his heart felt lost as it had the past month, since he had been separated from his master. His stomach was empty. They had run him away from his only source of food at the rest stop, so now it was road kill, throw outs, or nothing, as he tried his best to follow his desire to get home. Back where it was warm, dry, and he was never hungry.

Old Josh stopped under the bridge. At least the rain was not falling and he could just stretch out, off the road in the grass, rest his paws and legs. In a moment, he heard a voice. It wasn't his master's voice but it was warm, friendly and welcoming.

"Hey boy, looking for a place to sleep? Come on up here it is flat and warmer up here. Maybe you would like this old Big Mac I found back at the rest stop?" Old Josh almost crawled up the embankment, slowing as he reached the man. Driven by hunger and the need to hear a friendly voice, he had to make it to the top, he had to. Ben reached out and gave him the burger. Josh ate like it was his last meal. Then Ben pulled him under the make-shift blanket and they drew closer to one another. Soon the rain was gone, the cold left and sleep was wonderful.

Just two old travelers moving along Interstate 40 in Arizona. Now they enjoyed the comfort of one another and the harmony of their snoring.

On Thursday, The Arizona Daily Sun Newspaper reported a wanderer and his companion dog were found dead under an overpass near the Flagstaff exit. Death for both seemed to be of a natural causes. No additional information on either available.

Author's note: Nice to have someone to cross over with.

The Shattered Clock

It was almost time for class to end. Having completed his plan for the day, the teacher asked what time it was, from a student in the rear of the class room. Walter, sitting near where the clock was hanging on the wall, turned first to the clock then back to the teacher. Walter said, "Look for yourself. The clock is right there."

Pointing toward the wall clock, the teacher said, "From my position, I can't see it, Walter." The teacher asked the second time, "What time is it?" Walter responded, "Man, I ain't your time keeper. Get you some glasses so you can see."

"No smart mouth, Walter, just the time," the teacher replied. With that, Walter pulled the clock off the wall and threw it at the teacher. Lucky for the class, the bell rang and all of the students ran for the door.

As Walter reached the door, the teacher asked him to stay after the others had left. Walter stayed, the teacher reached to the floor, picked up the clock and put it on his desk. The teacher asked, "You can't tell time, can you, Walter?"

"Ain't none of your business, what I can and can't do," Walter responded. Then the teacher turned the clock face up and moved the hands, to ask, "What time is it, Walter?" Walter just stood there staring into space, and asked if he could leave.

"If you would like to learn to tell time, Walter, I will be at the community library on 12th Street, each night this week at 6:00 pm. I'll be glad to teach you both to read and tell time. Sure, now you can leave," the teacher spoke. Walter left the room. For two nights, the teacher waited until 7:00 pm at the library, and hoped that Walter would come in. The teacher had seen Walter, unknown to Walter, standing behind the bushes on both nights. When the teacher arrived, Walter just couldn't make the move. On the third night at 6:30 pm, Walter came into the library and said, "I ain't saying I can, or can't tell time, but I am here, so show me what you want me to know."

This began a two year journey between Walter and his teacher. Three nights each week, they met in the library. For three nights a week, they worked on homework, reading, math, and all the other quests a fifteen year old boy is involved with.

Walter didn't become an 'A' student, but he did pass for the first time in his school career. He graduated, got a good job with a big box store, and left his world of frustration behind. His former failures were broken into pieces like that old clock on a school room floor.

A dedicated teacher didn't see a shattered clock, but a broken boy.

A Big Chocolate Cake

Judy was one of those ladies that was always involved, but never noticed. If there was work to be done at church, she was involved in doing it. Prayers to be prayed, visits to be made, and cakes to cook. Judy was your lady.

Only a few times did anyone ever say anything about her work. Most of the time, it went unannounced and for the most part, it seemed to go unnoticed.

In time, Judy went to be with the Lord. She was not in her regular place, not doing all of the work, and not baking the cakes.

At the very next social, a nine year old child came running to his mother from the food line, and asked her, "Where is the big beautiful chocolate cake?" It was then that everyone remembered. It was Judy who had made those wonderful cakes. Now Judy was gone and so were her cakes. Maybe the preacher did not notice, maybe even some of the ladies, but a teary-eyed nine year old boy sure did notice that her work was not there.

Most good people never receive the good things that should be theirs in this world. But to be sure God noticed. Maybe He likes big Chocolate Cakes.

Old One Tusk

When I was teaching school, a small child gave me a small gift wrapped in white paper and asked that I not open it until the class was gone. When I tore open the package, I understood the reason. It was a one-tusk-missing elephant. It was not new, it had seen a lot of seasons but this child knew that I loved elephants. Since her family had no money, she had talked her mother into giving away a long used item from off their trinket shelf.

I wrote the family a thank you note. Later, when we returned from school holidays, that gift was on my desk, sitting on top of a beautiful glass mounting. The little girl had given me from her heart. I wanted her to understand that I had received it, with all of my heart.

Needless to say Old One Tusk, the little elephant mounted on the glass, was the hit of our returning day to school. Everyone wanted to know what it cost, if it was expensive, and who had given it to me. I explained that it was very valuable because the person who gave it to me treasured it and that is what makes a gift expensive.

I explained that it would not be polite to say who had given it, and in time, the questions stopped. But the child who gave it, never stopped smiling. From that day on, she was a great student always doing her best.

Some years later, I was able to return the gift to her. Even years later, I heard that she was a first grade teacher, married with children, and an 'Old One Tusk' was on her class room desk.

Well Done

*J*ames was different. He was several years older than I was, but he always enjoyed playing with me. In many ways, he acted much younger. Today, we would put James in a special class. They would have called him 'challenged'. In those days, they just sent him home, sometime in the third grade, and told him not to bother to come back to school.

James' older brother was smart, and did well in school. James lived in a world of cowboys and Indians, movies on Saturday, and playing with me, anytime his father came out to help my dad with things around the house.

Somewhere about the age of twelve, I realized that even though he was older, James was stuck in a world of childhood and all that goes with it. I liked him though. When his father died, my dad took James under his wings, gave him a job, and taught him how to take care of himself on his small salary. Dad would answer very simple questions put forth by James and with great patience, went over the same instructions, time after time.

As the years passed, James told my father that he had met a girl. James wondered if he could get married. Dad told him to bring her by, so he could meet her, and talk to them both. A few days later, James showed up with his girlfriend in a wheelchair. After months of guidance and counseling, James and his sweetheart married.

Dad helped James buy a small house, and got him a job with the city. For years, Dad watched over his needs. James' brother, who had all the great possibilities, died in prison. James and his wife in a wheelchair grew old together. While living a simple life, they were happy, healthy, and giving members of the community.

Later, we saw an old man pushing his wife down the street in a wheelchair. Both of them were laughing and rejoicing, as they journeyed to their little white home, where the love of God flowed out of the front door, down the street, and into all who knew them.

I believe I heard, "Well done, James!"

A Great Teacher and Encourager

As a small shy boy of nine, I met Mrs. Wilson, my fourth grade teacher. I thought she was the prettiest teacher I had ever seen. I was far too bashful to even be noticed in her class. In fact, I was the smallest person in the class.

During class, I never answered a question, never offered a remark, and stayed out of the way, very near the back of the room. I felt safe in not being noticed, so I made sure that I did not bring attention to myself. I didn't respond well to other children at that time, and seldom took part in any recess activity. For some reason, I felt very inferior and just wanted to be alone.

Mrs. Wilson must have noticed these traits in me, and decided to invest more than teaching in my life. Before class one day, she asked if I could do her a favor. I wasn't sure how to respond but nodded that I would. She told me that she had been collecting 'Blue Horse' notebook covers. When she got a certain number of these, and sent them in, she would receive a nice gift for our class. She said she needed me to count all of the covers, put them in stacks of 100, and give her a total count.

This thrilled me, I am not sure why, but I gladly completed the task. She told the class what a good job I had done and how proud all of us should be. She said our class would be receiving a new world globe because of my hard work, and their gifts of notebook covers. All of this was far outside her duties as a teacher, but somehow she knew that they were duties of her life and calling.

Teaching is a great and noble calling. Teachers invest so very much into the lives of our children. Like great soldiers, we owe them our honor and thanks.

Without knowing it, Mrs. Wilson became my first encourager. I have never forgotten her and will always be indebted to her.

October

Autumn

Halloween and Other Days

et me get on my old rags before I write this because I know I am going to have some tomatoes thrown at me for this blog. Why not read it all and do so with the understanding, that one of the beautiful things about our land, is that we do not all have to think alike.

I understand, for I have read, just as you have, all the 'stuff' written about Halloween and other days we observe. I can understand that many people do not wish to observe Halloween. Well, we really don't observe it, we just do it, feed our kids too much candy and make them look like, well, who knows what.

I know churches for example that will not use the name, 'Halloween', they call it something else. That is ok, but calling a horse a cow, does not change the fact that it is a horse. I also understand all the mystery that is supposed to surround this day, but in truth folks, that is not what we do today. No matter what it might have once been, that is not the day we have, not even in my lifetime. That is a long time ago! Has it been more than a night for candy, treats, and lots of pumpkins? Yes. Of course the eggs, now we can do away with the eggs. Besides, they cost too much.

Of course, some will say, look how it all started. I understand that but it is not what we do now. For example, I hate slavery. The man who wrote "Amazing Grace" was the Captain of a slave ship in his early years before he met the real author of Amazing Grace. That does not keep me from loving the song and wanting it to be played at my home-going. Don't get so tight that you always want to fight. Stand for truth, but don't invent a problem.

Same goes for Christmas. You are right, I love Christmas. Maybe it had a bad start. But boy, at 246 South Lindsey Street, it was the wonderful day of His birth and I got the presents. Hard to beat that. I also enjoy, not the best word, I observe, Easter. I know it had a tough start but we always knew that He, Jesus, would win.

Enjoy the days, supervise your children, and tell them the wonderful stories of Christmas and Easter. Try your best not to look like the spook you can be on Halloween.

Come by our church on October 31 and share in a great time of Trunk or Treat.

A New Ministry

A lady called to tell me that she came out of a store in Cookeville and saw a man standing with a sign which read, "Will work for food." As she passed him, she said she just could not hold it in. She said, "Why don't you get a job and go to work?"

"His response was immediate, 'Show me where one is and I will go to work'."

The lady told him she had some yard work, maybe a couple of hours' worth. She asked him what he would charge. He said, "How about supper?" She asked what kind of supper and he said a burger and fries. She told him to hop in the back seat and she would throw in a large coke.

The man did a great job. He was still doing work in the community for families she had called upon, and they were told that she had found a real worker. She priced his work at ten dollars an hour with a meal thrown in.

The lady went on to tell me that he went to church with her family on Sunday. She had another week of work lined up for him, new clothes were coming, and meals were always great. The mission, where he slept, found him a room where he could live.

The lady was weeping as she told me that she had always thought that people like him were just begging, not wanting to work. God had opened a door for a new ministry for her and her church. See, God is good.

Home

It was more than fifty years ago but I remember it like last week. I lived in the church's house, which was located next door, in the same yard with the church.

We'll call him Bob. He was about seven at the time and he spent a lot of time at my house. He lived in a small share cropper's house in the field across from me. Just out of nowhere he asked me one day, "Why do people say there is 'No Place Like Home'? I know lots of places I like better than home."

I searched for something to say for several minutes. I said something like, "Bob, when you are old enough to understand the difference between a house and home, then you will know what that saying means." He looked at me and said in a very mature voice, "I like both your house and your home more than mine."

Knowing nothing else to do, I hugged him and turned away.

This past October, I was in the same area of that long ago place, speaking at an association's meeting. I had some time to kill before I had to be at the meeting. I went by the church and house I had lived in over fifty years ago.

As I decided to visit the house across the road, to see if the family was still there. I discovered my former seven year old friend, now a grown man, with his own family. We spoke a few minutes. He said that he remembered me and we talked about long ago days.

As he turned and looked toward where he had lived before, he said with tears in his eyes, "Remember that question I asked you about home? I'm making real sure that my family knows that there is no place like home. Brother Ivan, I never had that place but I have it now and so do my children."

Knowing nothing else to do, I hugged him and turned away.

As I drove off, brushing back the tears, I thanked God that sometimes even in this life, things work out right. I praised Him for allowing me the desire to go backward for just a moment.

Blind Driver on Hwy. 13

Dr. Lawrence Steiner and I were headed home to Waynesboro from Florence, AL. We noticed a lady standing by her car on the shoulder of the south bound lane. We made a U-turn and pulled in behind her car to see if we could help.

As we approached her to ask if we could help, the lady looked frustrated and said, "I am out of gas." She continued to say, she had told the same to those two so-and-so preachers, whom she had called in Waynesboro. She had told them she was almost out of gas and had to go to see the doctor in Florence.

As she looked at us, she said, "You know how so-and-so preachers are, they do not help anyone but themselves." We stuttered a bit, told her we knew where there was a garage just down the road, and we would go to get her some gas. She said that would be nice but she didn't have any money. She did have an empty gas can in her trunk. We explained that we could handle the money but that the gas can would be great.

As we drove back toward the garage, we laughed at each other and wondered if we should tell her that we were also Preachers. Then we tried to guess the two Preachers she talked to in Waynesboro. We decided when we found out; we would make them split the cost of the gas.

We got the gas, put it in her tank, and helped her get the car started. Also, we gave her fifteen dollars and suggested she stop at the garage to fill up. Fifteen dollars does not sound like much, but remember gas was well under a dollar per gallon in those days.

After she thanked us, she said, "Sure is nice to meet some handsome, polite, and generous men. Too bad those so-and-so preachers couldn't be like you two nice looking men." We drove off in a bit of a hurry realizing that the lady not only had a bad mouth, she was also blind.

Who Failed Leadership 101?

Do you sometimes wonder what happened to leadership? Where did the men and women go, who understood the importance of moving in the right direction? What happened to the person who could take a stand that we did not agree with? Still at the end of the conversation, we would remain friends. When did leadership demand dictatorship?

I remember when I was young; we would go out to the sandlot and get up a ball game. Even when we disagreed with something the other person proposed, we reached a compromise and we played the game.

Today's leadership has stopped building friends on all sides of the choices. We have determined to be right even if it means leaving the sandlot silent, with no shouts of young voices having a great time. I believe it is time to listen, and hear the hearts of others. Share our own concerns with love, conviction, and reason.

I understand that there are times when we draw a line in the sand. Yet not over every issue, not every wish has to be filled and not all the wants have to be put in my bag.

Maybe it is time for our leaders to go to a ball game together, eat a 'Big Mac', take their families to Washington, and let the wives help build a family of Americans. Maybe a few afternoons of sandlot ball, with equal parts of both parties being on the teams, would help us realize that we are still one Nation, one People, with the greatest ability in the entire world.

We are just about ready to throw it all away because of our selfish attitudes.

I know that there is a group of men in both houses of both parties that meet each week for prayer. Let it be our prayer that their numbers will grow and their tribe increase. Turn off the 24/7 news and spend some time praying for our leaders to pass Leadership 101.

In The Mountains

A couple of years ago, I spent a week with the Smoky Mountains Resort Ministries. I worked with them as they ministered to thousands of people, who visited the area during the 'Leaf' time of the year. I assisted with the Fall Craft show, talking with vendors and visitors each day, from eleven until five. Since I enjoy talking, I had a great time. I met so many wonderful people and others, who did not quite make it.

One lady I helped had a lot of trouble walking. I ran some errands for her, as well as I watched her craft booth. She was depressed. Sickness does that to people. She had allowed it to turn her attention within. It did not allow her to reach out with her pleasant personality. We talked a lot. I think I left her a bit less depressed than when we first met. I spent some time in prayer for her each night. I just know the Lord is going to bring her more business, as well as more joy.

I met a lot of men who had served in our military, as well as a female, full bird Colonel. We talked about how difficult it had been for her to advance. She had met the different challenges that a mostly "male Army" offers to a female, trying to make it a career. We prayed together. She left with a belief that our meeting was no accident but a plan from our Lord.

Also, I spent some time with a man who had lost his leg in Vietnam. Because his leg was broken, they had removed it while he was in a prison camp. He gave our Lord the credit for being able to survive almost five years of imprisonment. It was a joy and privilege to speak and pray with him about our Lord.

Then, there was the newlywed couple, to whom I suggested they find and watch the movie, "Fire Proof". They returned the next day to let me know that they had purchased it, watched it, and were thrilled at the message. They have a real chance of making it to the finish.

There were people growing old and afraid, people worried about our nation, and those in so much debt, that the future seems impossible to face. Carlton, a young boy left behind by all the knowledge of this world, was thrilled that I let him touch my beard. I spent some time talking to him while his mother did a bit of shopping. She hugged me and almost cried as they left. Carlton waved all the way out of sight.

Nothing that 'changed the world' kind of week, but it was good for me. Those with whom my path crossed, I hope it was good for them also.

I Don't Mind Sharing

Robert and his family of five had been living with us for about a week. They had waited on a place to open for their family to live on our Baptist Children's Home Campus. Robert was a four year old. He was stretched out on the floor in our family room, with a bowl of cheerios and milk in front of him, as he ate his breakfast and watched TV.

Louie, our Cocker Spaniel, was stretched out beside Robert. As Robert took a bite, then Louie licked himself a nice bite also.

As I came in the room, I said, "Son, Louie is eating out of your bowl." Robert looked up at me and with those big eyes beaming, he said, "That's okay, sir, I got plenty and I don't mind sharing."

I'm sure I should have told Robert all the reasons that weren't good. However, Louie looked up and saw me. I walked over to the door to let him outside.

"Mister," Robert said, as he looked and pointed to the door of our pantry, "There is a lot of food in there. We are never going to be hungry." Then with those big eyes of a four year old, he looked at me and asked, "Sir, are you Jesus?"

I smiled, knelt down by him and said, "No, I'm not Jesus but He is the reason you came to live with us. He loves you and wants you to have a great home."

Robert just smiled real big and headed upstairs to his room. I walked to the back door and saw Louie stretched out on the porch, enjoying the morning sun, as his cheerios and milk digested.

I bowed my head and just wept before my God, who has given me so much that I can never be thankful enough and express it enough.

I love you Lord.

Dr. Billy Graham

When I visited New York World's Fair in 1964, it was filled with wonders for a young man from Tennessee just out of the Navy. I walked until my strong legs of youth were almost gone. Then I went to visit and sat awhile in the Billy Graham pavilion.

The pavilion was filled with pictures of crusades that Dr. Graham led, and cities where they planned to visit in the next couple of years. There was a place to sit down, get a soda and just rest, so I managed that very well.

About the time I decided to leave, I had a chance meeting with an evangelist, Merle Roselle, who I had first heard preach when I was in California. At the Balboa Park Baptist Church, Merle had led a revival when I attended there. I had gotten to visit with him and have a couple of meals along with a group of people from the church.

Merle hugged me, asked how I was doing, and wanted to know if I had seen Dr. Graham. I had not. Merle went on to say he was sure Dr. Graham was in. Merle told me to follow him and we went behind a false wall. He called the lady at the desk by name and asked if we could see Dr. Graham. She told him most assuredly. The two of us knocked on Dr. Graham's office door. Then we walked into the presence of one of the greatest men who has ever preached the 'Good News'.

Merle introduced me to the great man, Dr. Graham. As he stood, he shook my hand and then gave me a great big fellow-preacher hug. I was in Heaven.

Dr. Graham asked all about my family, my boyhood, and my dreams. When I left the room, I believed that I was really someone. I don't think I washed my hand for a week. After all, it had touched Dr. Graham.

Dr. Graham was so real, so personal, so unimportant to himself. I still remember leaving there with the full knowledge that Billy Graham was real. After all of these years, he has proved it so. What a man God made, when he made Dr. Billy Graham. We need more like him today.

November

Veterans and Thanks

Twenty-Five Thanksgiving Dinners

A judge in our small town gave me 25 turkeys to give to families that might not have a great Thanksgiving.

Man, I went crazy! It was going to be a beautiful day so I was off to give out 25 turkeys. The first house I went in changed my mind, for the lady of the house told me that she had never cooked a turkey.

After I told her to put it in the sink, and cover it with water, then I said it would be ready to cook the next day. She explained to me that she did not have running water in the house. Then she said how far up the hill she would have to go to get water. To put a nail in my coffin, she said neither she, nor any of her neighbors, had a pan large enough to cook it in.

Realizing I had to get my thinking cap on, I took the turkey, and told her I would be back the next day. I said I was sure she would have a wonderful Thanksgiving dinner.

After I rounded up several of our church ladies, I told them the whole story. They all got together, cooked the turkeys, and made all the fixings for a wonderful dinner. We all went back the next day to bring a fully cooked, complete Thanksgiving dinner for twenty five families.

As I learned, there is more than one way to cook a turkey. The best way during that week was to have some wonderful ladies have a ball cooking dinner for twenty five families, who had never had a turkey.

Great Thanksgiving that year, great.

Thanksgiving from My Youth

The sounds of Christmas were already in the air. The smells of food, as they were being cooked for a great feast of Thanksgiving, battled for the attention of our nose.

Before my family ever celebrated with a turkey, I was in college. We always had a couple of baked hens with all the trimmings. I don't remember if turkeys were too expensive, or not as available as today, or maybe mother had nothing large enough to cook one in. We just didn't have turkey.

Not that it mattered. We had a table so full that we were always able to eat for days on leftovers. The house was filled with family from the smallest grandchild to Mom and Dad. My entire family was always there, as we listened to the stories of days gone by, played in the yard, and fell asleep on the couch, chairs, and floor.

Until I was a senior in high school, we didn't have television. A family member entertained us. We came back to the table to snack for supper. One by one, all left our home at 246 South Lindsey Street. The sun fell from the sky, the night air became cold, and a reminder that winter was coming.

As I slept those nights, it was sleep of the innocent. I was full, warm, and snug in the bed of my youth. God carved the memory of those beautiful days in my heart.

Now in the time of my own winter, I find it warm to remember, to travel down those carved pathways and walk again those beautiful, full and wonderful days of Lindsey Street.

The Tears of the Lost

ome years ago a lady came into my office and poured out to my secretary and I. This was a number of years ago. I don't have a secretary at Byrdstown.

The lady told us she had fallen so many times, broken the hearts of her parents, and abandoned her children. Even though she had yet to turn forty, she could not name her husbands in any order, even with the help of her fingers. She said she had heard me preach and that I had looked across the audience and said that God loved her. She knew I had to be talking about someone else, that she was certain that God could not love her. She talked in a whisper because she said even to mention it, she was afraid that God would somehow punish her before she could leave the office.

My secretary handed me my Bible turned to Psalm 139. I read David's great praise to God for loving him in spite of knowing him. I told her of the woman at the well and how God had used her to change a city. I told of the woman who came with tears and perfume to anoint the feet of Jesus, too sinful to stand before him. How John, when he heard the voice of God, fell before His feet as though he, John, was dead. I told how God used a big fish to teach a man, who refused to serve Him, how to change the history and destiny of a great city. I then told her that David had caused murder, committed adultery, and lost the joy of his family, but was still loved by God and called the apple of His eye. David had said that God not only knew him but loved him.

She shed the tears of a broken and saddened child, as my secretary and I prayed for her. With tears flowing with the force of rain, she wept her sorrow before God and gave Him all that she could, the years that were left.

Is it not wonderful, marvelous, glorious, and beyond understanding how much God loves us, even when we are who we are?

Let Him Make it to the End

A s he looked at all the holiday food on the table, the tears would not leave. He listened as his nephew said the prayer and the tears still came.

He excused himself, walked out of the kitchen door into the back yard. He pulled his pipe out of his pocket, stopped a moment, and lit it. Then he walked to the edge of the yard and sat down on the bench he had put there when he had been a young man, and tears never came.

He looked back toward the house. He had lived there for a long time. In fact, a life time. It was from that house that he had left for the Navy, flight school, and Vietnam. It was in that house that both of his parents had died while he was gone.

They never knew that he was a 'guest' of the North Vietnamese Army. Those years had aged them, crushed them, and before his terror ended, they were taken in a twist of events called an accident.

He remembered those five years of his own personal terror, the loss of faith, the regaining of faith, and the desire to make it to the end. No matter how long that would take, he would make it to the end.

His sister had learned three weeks after their parent's death, that he was somewhere in a place called Hanoi, alive. Hopefully, if all the diplomatic chess games worked with America and the enemy, he would come home.

That had been over forty years ago, yet that first day seemed to him like only this morning. The house was empty that first day. His sister and her husband had kept it, repaired it, and left it vacant for the day he would return.

He tried marriage but was terrible at it. He loved but never accepted the love of his wife. No children, no success. He had just lived in the house, worked at the simplest of jobs he could live with, and made it, one day to the next.

For the rest of the world, that war was long forgotten, the enemy now friends. The pains of those five years, not believed by most, were considered deserved, by some. For him, in the deep of his night, he heard the silent sounds of that cell, smelled the filth of the place, and saw the hate of those who held him. He still felt the pain of bones unset and deep cuts untreated. To him, the night never really ended, the prison was never left, and he had yet to make it to the end.

Today, all that food on the table, which his sister, her children and grandchildren had cooked. It was wonderful. For a moment, he remembered the empty bowls that were shoved under his door, and the hard dark bread placed in them, that were to serve as the meal of the day.

Lt. Searcy Belton, USN, never left his prison, never made it to the end. The price he paid was not in years, but in a lifetime. Unlike the storybook tales that always end with 'they lived happily ever after', his book never ended. Somehow in some way, we ask our Heavenly Father to heal his wounds when He greets him in glory.

Preparing For Thanksgiving

ost of you are busier than a one-arm-paper-hanger in a wind storm when trying to get ready for Thanksgiving. Make sure all you need is on hand to complete your Thanksgiving dinner. Know the football schedule so you won't have family members jumping up to check on the game. Make your shopping list for Black Friday, with time and places you need to be. Family members and friends you must call. It is going to be a busy day. Now I come along and add to your list.

Lead your family on Thursday, and be thankful for Sgt. William Story, standing watch on a hill in Afghanistan so that our lunch might go well. Be thankful for Lt. Page Whitehouse, flying her helicopter into harm's way, to bring out the wounded, even the wounded enemy. Be thankful for Petty Officer Steve Chandler, aboard the USS Florida, deep under the ocean, where not even those who know can tell anyone. His duty of silence makes our enemy aware that they can never win in a nuclear war against America.

Of course, there is Pvt. George Simmons, somewhere near the neutral zone in South Korea standing his post, keeping the honor of America, for whom we are thankful. Serving as duty officer, aboard a ship at sea, is Lt. John Fisher, for whom we are also thankful. Another is Sgt. Marvin Suiter, in a ditch looking across the landscape, hoping the enemy will not come today.

A mother's son or daughter, a wife, a husband, or a father, are all around the globe. These men and women keep watch today, not of a Football game, not for a great meal with their family, but somewhere on the edge of conflict and terror.

A police officer, a fireman, a medic, a trooper, all away from home, missing family and friends, in order for all of us to laugh. We are thankful for all of these dedicated people, in order for us to have a wonderful meal, enjoy a lot of football, eat too much, and fall safely asleep on our couch in this land of the free and home of the brave.

Let us give our thanks to God and His abiding care, upon one and all, that make this day free for each of us.

Long, Long Ago

On Lexington Street, in the second house from the corner where Camden meets Lexington, I was born long, long ago. It was on a Thursday, November 11. The world in which I arrived was so very different. Less than half of the people had a phone or car, and no one had even heard of television.

My two younger sisters did not know that mother was going to have a baby. They were both over the age of nine. In fact, my sister, Peggy thought that Dr. Brown had brought me in the black bag, which he had when he came to take care of my birth.

Those were innocent years. Several people on the street had Ice Boxes, not refrigerators. Our rent was $10.00 a month, so we moved to the house on the corner, a larger, much nicer but still only $10.00. The year I turned four, we purchased a home at 246 South Lindsey Street, where I would live until I left home.

The price of the house was $1,375. That is not a mistake, one thousand three hundred and seventy five dollars. I grew up with three older sisters, one married by the time I was four. We listened to the radio as a family at night, like it was a great magic box. On Saturdays, we went to the 'Moving Picture Show'. Go figure, just the kids. Mom and Dad would shop.

We ate together at home with very few exceptions. When we went to Dyersburg to see my grandparents in their home, I am sure I was a junior in High School before we ate in a restaurant. On Sundays, we went to the church, Calvary Baptist Church. Our church was at the corner of Tomlin and Lexington, and we seldom missed.

Knowing that I was loved by the people in that church, I grew up loving church. Sometimes it seems like a very long time ago, for our world has changed so very much. As a community, East Jackson and the whole of the city prayed for our men in 'the service' during the Second World War. We wept with our neighbors when we learned that one of our 'boys' was being shipped out. Too many times, we wept pools of tears for those who would never come back to Jackson.

We wrote real letters, walked to a friend's house and just 'stayed' a while. If it was a real emergency, we would make a long distance call. Otherwise, we put a three cent stamp on an envelope and mailed a letter. We didn't seem like we were always in a rush, and time seemed to move so slowly.

Now after long, long ago, time moves swiftly. Now I am old and yesterday is forever gone. I am grateful for my yesterday, for it gave me a family, a community, and a church that shares the knowledge.

In Jesus, I would really never grow old.

The Birds Have Their Trees

*D*avid sat on the park bench in Franklin Square and watched as the young mother talked with her daughter. The mother looked to be about 50 years old, but he was sure she was still in her 20's. She was dressed in several sweaters, all worn but clean, and had at least three pair of pants held on her body by a rope. Her head was covered, with swollen eyes, and her voice was tearful as she spoke to her four year old child. He heard her explain that they would not have a tree this Christmas, where they lived in the back of the broken panel truck. The truck was parked in an abandoned lot, near a once but now closed warehouse. There would be no room for a tree.

David wondered what turn of events had rocketed this pair of lost souls into such despair and sorrow. What happened, who was at fault? Did it really matter? Here she was and so it was. The Salvation Army officer stopped to speak to them. David knew and felt for her circumstances.

As David heard the mother talk with Salvation Army about choices, he understood as the mother pled for a real plan to give her and her daughter a chance at life. The Salvation Army officer shook his head, said he would try, prayed and walked away.

David caught up with the officer, and asked him a lot of questions. The two spent a long time at the Star Bucks across the street. David left the officer, as he shook his head in unbelief. David handed him an envelope, shook his hand, and went back to the park bench in the square.

David listened when the Salvation Army officer returned a few hours later, to talk to the mother and child, still on their bench at the park. The officer explained that he had a job for the woman at the Star Bucks across the street.

The mother raised questions about child care, clothes, and a place to live. Salvation Army explained that there was a new program and she could be the pilot mother for its launch. There was an efficiency apartment about eight blocks away where she and her daughter could live for the next six months. There was also money for clothes for both of them, with child care at the National Christian Church, just down the street.

With the starting salary, the lady could not afford the apartment. However, within six months, there would either be more salary, or another place to live. The mother looked startled, began to weep, and wrapped her arms around the

Salvation Army Officer. She let the flood of joy wash the sidewalk beneath her feet.

David wiped his eyes, as he looked at the large tree in the square and said, "My Father's birds have their trees. This child and mother needs theirs." David spoke to the weeping mother, the excited child, and the smiling Salvation Army worker, as he left Franklin Square.

December

Christmas

Christmas Eve

ell it is here, that last day before Christmas, the malls are open, and the stores are hoping for a great day in retail. The children are delighted that Santa will be here as the night falls on this day before Christmas.

I have always liked to purchase at least one gift on this day. It just seems the right thing to do. I know many of you are ready for it to all be over. I say enjoy the day, eat an apple, watch a ball game, take a nap, and tell the children a great story. It is the only day we have just before Christmas and it too will soon be but a shadow.

Carole and I are going out to dinner with some friends tonight. Then to bed, waking tomorrow to attend our worship service with our friends and family at First Baptist in Byrdstown.

It will be a beautiful service, for it is the birthday of The King.

Be sure to make room for the worship hour on Christmas. It will provide a good break. Jesus will be blessed that you would celebrate His Birthday, in an hour on His birthday.

Tuck the children in, maybe read the story of the King first. Then let them wake you before the sun, in order to give shouts of excitement that Christmas is here and Santa has paid them a visit.

Have a blessed day and we will see you at church at 11 AM. If you can't attend, then tune in on your computer by going to **www.kingofkingsradio.com**.

Christmas Day Service

Our worship service on Christmas Day, wow! I cannot tell you how pleased and blessed I felt. Shirley Scott and Judy Sterns opened our service with a powerful song. Then we enjoyed our people singing followed by Breanna and Bailey Amonett, in a beautiful time of three great songs. Wow!

We were ready, we shared the message. Then as we observed the Lord's Supper, Cathy Mullins did three more songs to fit that beautiful service.

Last night I received a number of emails from people telling me how they were blessed, and how the word of God had really spoken to them in the service. Some shed tears, some smiles of joy, others gave reminders of other days, and loved ones, gone on before them.

Thank you, First Baptist Family of Byrdstown, for supporting the service and providing our church with the joy of Christmas Day.

I am sure that across our area so many churches had the same blessed event as we did. God seemed so real, the troubles of this life so covered by His blood and the joy of His promise of life forever. We close the year on a grand note. We open The New Year on a grand hope.

It Feels Good Tonight

David loved Christmas! Even though this was his first Christmas, he had fallen in love with it at first sight. The lights, everywhere there were lights, the music, the food, what was not to like, even the shoppers. It was a wonderful time and he enjoyed each moment.

David stood to the side inside the store, watching the children line up to tell Santa what they wanted for Christmas. They were excited, some bashful, some cried. Many of them hugged the white bearded man and ran quickly back to their parents.

David heard Bobby asking Santa for a Remote Controlled Fire Truck, with a long ladder on the back. David saw to the side, in a crowd of parents, Bobby's mother was trying to get Santa's attention and shaking her head "no". But no matter what Santa suggested, Bobby came back to the fire truck.

David watched Bobby's mother count out money for the picture of Bobby and Santa, which the clerk handed her. It seemed to David that it had taken most of her money. She clutched the picture, and placed it in her bag. She followed Bobby as he dragged her to the stack of Remote Controlled Fire Trucks in the center aisle.

David saw her look with almost tearful eyes at the $69.95 price tag on the sign. Then she gently directed Bobby to another part of the store. David got the attention of a clerk. Then he gave Bobby's mother a box with the fire truck in it, and also handed her a large box of Legos. David asked if she could get it wrapped in a hurry. She assured him it would be done in a flash.

With the package in hand, David went out to the front of the store. He asked the Santa, who was collecting funds for something, to give the box to the lady coming out with the small boy in tow. With that, David placed a ten dollar bill in the Santa's pot, and stood against the wall of the building.

Santa handed the box to the lady and she jumped, as though she was afraid. Santa said, "Not to worry, Ma'am, this is a gift from Santa. Please take it but you can't open it until Christmas morning." She started to talk, but Santa said, "On your way now, Ma'am. Santa is very busy. Merry Christmas and Ho, Ho, Ho!"

David smiled as he watched the mother and son look at the wrapped gift as they walked toward the car. Not a big thing he thought. It won't change the world. No one will know a year from now, but it sure does feel good tonight.

Christmas Blessings

Remembering 1954, there were many families with needs. We were one of those many. But I remember the love we shared at Christmastime. Gifts were almost non-existent. But we had food from the cellar, put up from the large garden Mom and the boys worked.

Bad times, but good times, too. Know what I remember most? Being thankful for the warm wood stove in the living room. That bedroom, with the snow blowing through the cracks, was mighty cold.

A body appreciates the blessings of today a bit more. In 1954, he saw the light of the moon shining through the bedroom window, and felt the snow blowing from just below the window sill.

Even then, we were blessed and I knew it. Know what I miss most? Mom. On the really difficult days, and there are still a few, I long to be held by her and squeezed as she often did, yes, as late as 1954.

Mary Pondered

When the shepherds left the manger scene, the Bible says that, "Mary kept all these things and pondered all them in her heart." (Luke 2:19 NKJV)

We can be sure, I think, that Mary had many such moments before the birth of Christ. We celebrate for Mary, the honor given to her, to bring the flesh born body of Jesus into the world.

Mary had no way to understand all that was taking place in her life. Mary visited Elizabeth and the moment Mary walked into the house, Elizabeth knew. Elizabeth knew that the baby within Mary was her Lord.

No one can know all that Mary went through in those months. Mary and Joseph could not celebrate as our couples do today, waiting for their child to be born. The neighbors did not make over Mary. In fact, I am sure that most felt that Mary and Joseph had broken their vows. They were sinners. The months were not spent in joy but in confusion. They knew the truth but no one else would believe the truth.

It would not be until the empty tomb that people would know, and believe. Even then, many still would not accept this wonder of wonders, this gift to each of us. One, who owed no debt, paid the debt which we all owe, and no one but Christ could pay.

Mary pondered, yes, many times and in many ways. Mary's son, God's gift to each of us, brought many tears and countless rumors to His parents.

Salvation is not free. God gave us His Son but the joys which we have over our children, Joseph and Mary were not able to share with their friends and neighbors. Salvation cost this family many tearful nights. It cost Christ His Glory, while He walked among men.

Maybe we should each say thank you, God, for your gift. Thank you, Joseph and Mary, for obeying God.

Just a Boy Again

As I stood in the checkout line, I hoped that the lady, with a hundred or more items, would soon be through. It looked to me like she was trying to purchase something from every department in the store.

Of course, she had coupons, gift certificates, and a due bill. Then she made a ten minute search for the money she needed to complete her purchase. It was a real experience to watch someone purchase three buggies of items. The clerk wished her a nice weekend, looked at my three items and smiled. The clerk said, "Nothing like getting behind Mrs. Russell, and she does that every week."

As I smiled, I said, "She must have a large family, plus a lot of money!" The clerk laughed and said, "She will bring half of it back the next day. She just likes to shop." We both laughed.

The young man behind me said, "Don't I know you?"

I turned and looked at him and had no memory of his face. "Not sure," I said. "I am a Baptist Preacher and have preached at a lot of places. Maybe you saw me somewhere like that."

The young man paid for his purchases and followed me to the door. Then he said, "You were Christmas, when I was nine." I looked confused and he went on, "My dad died when I was nine. My sister and I had no Christmas that year. You were the Pastor at the church down the street. On the day before Christmas, you brought gifts and food to our house from your church."

I asked him where this was. When he told me, the past returned, and I remembered. Even though it had been over thirty years, a small glimpse returned.

The young man told me how much it had meant to his family. He told me his mother remarried, and they had moved. He now had a family of his own. Then he reached out and hugged me and said, "I don't remember your name but I will never forget your voice, and that best of all the days of Christmas long, long ago."

My age didn't show as I walked to my car. God had just given me a wonderful gift and I was a boy again just for a moment.

Christmas at Point Loma

On Friday, December 12, 1958, I had arrived in San Diego. It was my first Christmas away from family and away from Jackson, Tennessee. The palm trees made into 'Christmas Trees' did not impress this West Tennessee boy with his memories of cedar trees. Palm trees left something missing from Christmas.

Since I was the new man on the duty roster, I pulled Christmas duty on that Thursday of 1958. Sometime that weekend, I went looking for something to do. I made my way to The Point Loma National Cemetery.

Standing there looking across that beautiful green bed, with its white markers pointing to the sky, I felt a sense of home. Looking back, I am sure it was because of my love for those who had served our country.

At Point Loma, you look across the hillside of the green grass, dotted with the white markers, into the great blue of the Pacific Ocean. It is a beautiful sight and a great reminder of the price that so many have paid for our freedom.

There was a lady and her young son of about seven. I was caught up in my own thoughts and did not notice the two. Until the boy, seeing me in my dress blues, came running over to me and asked with great seriousness, "Did you know my dad?"

Standing, not sure what to say, his mother answered for me, as she told the boy not to bother me. She told her son that I would not have known his father. I stooped down and asked the child to show me his father's grave.

As I read with pride, "Chief Petty Officer Dan Raymond Sharp, 1919 – 1952", I saluted his grave. I put my hat on his son, and saluted the boy as well.

That day, as I left that beautiful and holy ground with tears, my heart was very proud and thankful, for all those who made the day possible for me.

Trees of Christmas

O n the first Saturday of December, Tom Stewart, who worked for my dad, would get the company truck and come by. Tom would pick up Dad and me so that we could all go out on Christmasville Road to a friend's farm. There we cut down Christmas trees for all of our family and many of our friends.

We always chose cedar trees. Until I joined the Navy and went to California, I had never seen any other type of tree used for Christmas.

Dad would always let me pick out a tree for our house. I would always choose the largest tree that would stand tall in our living room.

We returned as the sun was falling from the sky. We delivered the trees to all of those who had asked for one. Then we went home, and ate supper. We also built a stand so that our tree would be upright in our living room before the day came to a close.

Later, we all gathered on Sunday after church, to put the lights and trimmings on the tree. We used ice sickles, made from foil, along with a lot of artificial snow. In those days, if one light went out on the string, then all the lights on that strand would also go out. It was my job to find the bad light and replace it with a new light. That was often a major job.

During the war years, we could not purchase new lights. Dad knew a way to make the old bulbs, if not glow, they still carried the circuit and keep the other lights burning. Mother always called "foul", and say that Dad was going to burn the house down. Somehow, we made it through those years and so did the house.

Life at 246 South Lindsey Street was good, full of love, adventure, tears, joys, hopes, and the launching platform for a little boy into manhood.

The Way We Are

As I sat in the back of our Byrdstown auditorium and enjoyed the Christmas Play presented by our children, I could not help but be very impressed. I was impressed with the stage, the boys and girls, and Shawna Rich who had put it all together. The weather was terrible, cold, dark and just bad, but the auditorium was filled with moms, dads, and entire families of different members of our cast.

The children took their parts very seriously. Even when the lead character got sick and had to be replaced at the last moment, the child who stepped forward for the task did an incredible job.

Starting on Friday, everyone had called and told me how no one could come and how it would be a real washout for the children. I listened and prayed and decided that the best move was no move at all, but to go on with the play, "The True Meaning of Christmas."

As I enjoyed the production, I realized that we were expressing the title of the play, as the full house of guests was saying, "These are our kids, and we love our kids. So bad weather or not, the show must go on and we will support even our smallest child."

That is the way we are in Byrdstown. We love our families, and we love our extended families, for that is what Christmas is all about. God desiring us to be a part of His family. God calling each one of us to love one another, because He loves all of us so very much.

Christmas 1954

During my senior year in high school, I was a student, selling Christmas items door to door. I was unprepared for what I saw when the door was opened. A one room house, filled with the smell of smoke from the open bucket of burning coals. Around the wall were six small children, dirty, poorly dressed and poorly fed, eating bread dipped in syrup, using the tops of the syrup cans for plates.

As I spoke to the lady, I started to mention what I was selling, but paused long enough to catch a glimpse of the despair, poverty, and hopelessness of the moment. I told her I was with Santa and wished to know what she needed for Christmas. She looked at my young white face in a tone of shock and uncertainty. I said, "I really am serious, I would really like to know what you need for Christmas." That was the start of one of the best Christmas Seasons I shall ever know.

When I entered the house with caution and some reservation, the children looked at me with wide eyes of wonder. A small one came and hugged my leg. I was surprised and a bit shaken. Remember this was West Tennessee in the 1950's. It was a different world. I am sometimes surprised that God did not remove all of us for our actions and attitudes. That is a message for another day. God is merciful even when we are not.

The mother said they did not have anything in the house to eat and very little coal left. Since I was 16, I was more interested in why there was no tree and no Christmas decorations. Time would answer that question. I said I knew where to get food and I thought I could get some coal.

Our home at 246 South Lindsey Street was raided for food, and I got coal from the place where my father worked. I headed back to the smoke and children-filled, one-room house. This was going to be a different Christmas!

That Christmas, I had worked hard and planned to make enough money to purchase a sport coat that I had seen Rock Hudson wear in a movie. It had leather patches on the elbows. I liked that coat.

As I got a small tree from back of my house, some lights from my brother-in-law, and purchased some other items for the tree, I made my way to Jackson's 'New York store', where I knew I could get some great toys. My father's 1948 Dodge was filled to overflow, as I parked in front of my now familiar, new friend's home.

The children popped through the door like a soda being shaken up, when they heard me close the car door. Never had so many hands clutched so many packages. The mother stood and smiled in a wondering way at the then slim, tall, very white boy. Her name was Marilee. I asked what she wanted for Christmas and she said quietly, "I've got it."

It was cold that December day in 1954. It was cloudy and dark, everywhere except over that small house, with smoke coming out of the top of an open window. With six bright, beautiful children all speaking at once, in wonder, at to what as in the packages.

There might even have been a small heavenly light over the roof. Herman Lindsey, owner of the 'New York store', had told me to come back, if I needed anything else. I noticed that the total he charged for the toys was a lot less than I expected. I went back to the store and asked him if he had some things to cook in, and also a stove that would stick out the window so the house would not be so full of smoke. He said for me to come back the next day and he would see what he could gather.

That next day we loaded his truck with a bed, several mattresses, cooking items, and a brand new stove with a chimney for the window. This time, the entire street turned out to help us unload the truck.

Mr. Lindsey and I walked from the house with a bit of spunk in our step. It had been a great Christmas and it was only December 23rd. I thanked Mr. Lindsey, gave him what money was left, then turned and hugged him around his neck. I learned later that Mr. Lindsey returned with his truck loaded with toys and gave them to children up and down the street on Christmas Eve.

I also realized later that Herman Lindsey was Jewish. But Mr. Lindsey knew who his neighbor was.

I never did get that patched coat, and I never missed it. I never talked with Mr. Lindsey again. The store closed some years later and I lost contact with the family. But that Christmas of 1954 was wonderful.

Lightning Source UK Ltd.
Milton Keynes UK
UKHW040629260120
357622UK00001B/8